Flusche, Della M
Forgotten females

DATE DUE

APR 6 '94			
MAR 10 '99			

FORGOTTEN

FEMALES

FORGOTTEN FEMALES:
Women of African and Indian Descent in Colonial Chile, 1535-1800

Della M. Flusche
Eastern Michigan University
and
Eugene H. Korth
University of Detroit

Blaine Ethridge — Books
13977 Penrod Street   Detroit, Michigan 48223

Please write for a free annotated catalog of books on Latin America, ethnicity, bilingual education and bilingual books for children.

Printed in the United States of America.

Library of Congress
Cataloging in Publication Data

Flusche, Della M.
    Forgotten females: Women of African and Indian
    Descent in Colonial Chile, 1535-1800

    Bibliography: p.
    Includes index.
    1. Women, Black—Chile—History. 2. Indians of South
America—Chile—Women—History. 3. Indians of South
America—Chile—Mixed bloods—History. 4. Women—
Chile—History. I. Korth, Eugene H. II. Title.
F3285.B53F48 1983   920.72′0983   82-24269
ISBN 0-87917-085-9

Dedicated to the women
whose story is recounted here.

Contents

Preface

Studies of race, ethnicity, and class in colonial Spanish America have traditionally emphasized the several separate social groups with scant differentiation regarding the sexes. Recently, however, scholars have begun to examine the distinctly female aspects of the colonial experience in greater detail. It is the purpose of this brief monograph to contribute to these efforts. To maintain a sharp focus, the subject matter is confined to nonwhite women in colonial Chile.

Manuscript materials, published documents, colonial chronicles, general histories, monographic treatments, and scholarly journals have all been utilized to draw Afro-Chilean, Indian and *mestiza* women out from obscurity. These sources reveal that females of inferior social status predictably did most of the ordinary "women's work" of the colony but received little recognition for their efforts. This was especially true of poor whites whose contributions to the well-being of the realm were consistently ignored not only in the documents of the time but in subsequent accounts also. Women of color, whether of African, Indian, or mixed blood parentage, fared considerably better in this regard than their white counterparts. The fact that they were frequently the subject of legislative action, of physical abuse and exploitation, of property transactions or manumission in the case of slaves, or of deathbed dispositions of various kinds meant that their names were often preserved in the official and private records of the period. They thus escaped the anonymity attached to the amorphous mass of poor whites. Color in this case proved to be an ironic advantage.

Since Spaniards went to great lengths to categorize persons by race, the question of color looms large in contemporary records which speak not only of blacks and Indians but also of the mixed blood castes. Because of this and the emphasis on gender in the Spanish language, we have found it appropriate to utilize Spanish terms as well as English equivalents for the several different ethnic groups.

For the benefit of readers whose knowledge of colonial Chile may be limited, the text begins with an introduction that explains pertinent

PREFACE

terminology and provides background on political, social, and economic features of the colonial period from 1535 to the early 1800s. The respective sections and chapters devoted to nonwhite women include analyses of their activities, measures enacted in their defense, abuses perpetrated against their rights, their resistance to exploitation, and their contributions to the economic development of the Long Land. A profile of an Inca princess, who came to Chile as the wife of a governor, serves to further accent the diversity of the nonwhite experience. A brief conclusion rounds out the book.

While we accept full responsibility for the contents of this small volume, we are indebted to our families, colleagues, and friends, especially Charles E. Ronan, S.J., who encouraged and assisted us during its preparation. We are also grateful to the Newberry Library for a research fellowship and to Eastern Michigan University and the University of Detroit for sabbatical leaves and grants-in-aid. As a glance at the bibliography will show, the book could not have been written without the efforts of other Latin Americanists, particularly past and present Chilean historians and archivists who rightfully enjoy international renown for their outstanding scholarship.

Della M. Flusche
Eastern Michigan University
Ypsilanti, Michigan

Eugene H. Korth
University of Detroit
Detroit, Michigan

Introduction

The Kingdom of Chile, bordering on the Pacific ocean and claiming the trans-Andean province of Cuyo as part of its territory until 1776, was a remote outpost of the Spanish Empire.[1] Although technically a part of the viceroyalty of Peru, Chile experienced little effective control from the viceregal authorities in Lima. More immediate power rested in the hands of a royally-appointed high court (*audiencia*) and a governor resident in Chile. The latter, when formally designated as *presidente* of the audiencia, could preside over the court, located initially in Concepción and later in the capital city of Santiago, but not necessarily participate in judicial proceedings. In his capacity as captain general, the governor served as commander-in-chief of the military forces engaged in the Araucanian war on the southern frontier. *Corregidores* (district administrators and magistrates) and city councils (*cabildos*) carried out routine regional and local functions. Protectors of Indians and administrators of Indian villages had a certain supervision over Indian affairs. Because of the close ties between Church and State, churchmen often exerted political as well as religious and moral influence. In far away Castile, the crown and the Council of the Indies received reports and petitions from officials and individuals, enacted legislation applicable to the distant colony, and exercised final jurisdiction over court cases which had been appealed to Spain. The Hapsburg monarchs of the sixteenth and seventeenth centuries established this pattern of government which endured with some modifications into the eighteenth-century Bourbon era.

The general characteristics of society in colonial Chile were not markedly different from those found in other Spanish American realms. A predominantly white upper class, including *peninsular* immigrants from Spain and their hispanized descendants born in America known as creoles (*criollos* and *criollas*), claimed precedence and prerogatives. Regardless of their place of birth, whites (*blancos, blancas*) within the elite circles identified themselves as Spaniards. Although frequently in debt, upper class Chileans enjoyed some degree of affluence. Since the color bar was not insurmountable, nonwhites occasionally gained acceptance in the elite groups. Those who did so were usually prominent Indians (*indios, indias*) and castes of mixed racial origins, especially *mestizos* and *mestizas* (male, female Euro-Indians). Fewer opportunities for upward social mobility were available to persons of African ancestry, whom the historian, Leslie B. Rout, Jr., designates as Negroids and Afro-Chileans, thereby encompassing blacks, mulattoes, and the offspring of black and Indian parents.[2] The middle and lower social and economic levels included whites, blacks, (*negros, negras*), Euro-Africans (*mulatos, mulatas*), Afro-Indians (*zambos, zambas*), Indians, and Euro-Indians. Throughout society, status depended not only on race but also on such disparate criteria as parentage, lifestyle, religious orthodoxy, freedom or bondage, occupation, and income.

The colonial economy drew some support from the mining of gold and copper but rested more firmly on livestock and agrarian commodities from ranches (*estancias, haciendas*) and small farms (*chacras, chácaras*). Artisans produced many utilitarian articles for the home market while imports provided luxury items for the fortunate few who could afford them. Small shops handled retail sales. In financial transactions, Chileans used several types of currency that understandably fluctuated in value. The gold *peso*, or *castellano*, equivalent to 450 *maravedís*, was a common monetary unit in the sixteenth century but soon gave way to the silver peso composed of 8 *reales*.

Within this political, social, and economic framework, nonwhite women individually and collectively assumed active and passive roles which made a difference to themselves and their contemporaries. As builders of the past, they helped construct the foundations of the present nation. It is their record which now concerns us.

PART I
AFRO-CHILEAN WOMEN

The importance of Afro-Chilean women in the formation of colonial Chile can scarcely be exaggerated. From the beginning, blacks, mulatas, and zambas participated in the foundation, growth, and development of the realm.

The presence of black people in the earliest Spanish expeditions from Peru to Chile is well documented, and historians mention that Diego de Almagro's slave Margarita accompanied his expeditionary force in 1535. When Almagro returned to Peru from his failed mission to conquer the southern land, he fought and lost a battle against the Pizarros, fell into their hands, and was condemned to death. While in prison awaiting execution in 1538, he confirmed an earlier promise to manumit Margarita. Although her formal emancipation was delayed almost a year, the freedwoman eventually became a shopowner in Peru and endowed a chaplaincy to provide prayers for the soul of Almagro and his followers.[1]

While Margarita demonstrated her initiative and assimilation into Peruvian society, another woman, Juana de Valdivia, who may have been a black or mulata slave, attracted notice in Chile as the wife of the black conquistador, Juan Valiente. Despite his legal status as a slave and harassment by his owner, Juana's husband rose to prominence in the nascent colony. Valiente had journeyed to Peru from Mexico, joined the Almagro expedition to Chile, returned in the 1540s with the conquistador Pedro de Valdivia as a cavalryman, and became an *encomendero* (recipient of a grant of Indians). Much less is known about his wife, but the fact of their marriage was acknowledged in the writ of *encomienda* (grant of Indians) dated 1550. Governor Valdivia mentioned his comrade's military record and remarked that Juan also merited the encomienda because he was "married and . . . maintained his household, wife, and person with all honor." This was a standard phrase routinely employed when married men obtained encomiendas. But Juana's husband was an uncommon man whose accomplishments earned him extraordinary recognition before his death at the hands of the Araucanians in 1553 left her a widow with the responsibility of

1

rearing their son.[2]

The small number of Negroid people who entered Chile with the early expeditions from Peru grew larger as the new colony developed. A few persons of African ancestry came throughout the colonial period as servants of wealthy immigrants or in the retinues of royal officials. For example, the black slave woman Leonor, who had been born in Seville, was brought to Chile where she belonged to Antonio Tarabajano for a time. Her new owner, Antonio's son-in-law, Agustín de Briceño, sold her to the merchant, Lázaro García, for 320 gold pesos in 1564, when she was approximately 30 years old.[3] Somewhat earlier the conquistador, Alonso de Córdoba, who was returning to Chile from Spain with his wife Olalla Hernández and their children in the 1550s, petitioned the crown for a license to take not only 20 of their relatives as immigrants but also 2 black men and 2 black women as servants.[4]

It is possible that some Negroid women who worked on the ships that plied the Pacific eventually took up residence in Chile. In 1591 Viceroy García Hurtado de Mendoza, a former governor of Chile, prepared a list of instructions for the commander of a coast guard patrol charged with protecting the waters from Peru to Chile from pirates. The officer was to make sure that a high level of morality was maintained and take steps to see that public sins were not committed. Specifically, no concubines were to be allowed on the vessels. The viceroy thought that shipboard concubinage was mainly caused by the presence of black female servants and ordered the naval commander to see to it that the fewest possible number of black women were on the ships.[5] What the viceroy failed to note was that these women, who worked as cooks and laundresses, contributed to imperial defense.

How many, if any, black women settled in Chile because of such voyages is unknown. Since Pacific naval operations were sporadic, the number was surely not large. However, some Negroid persons journeyed to Chile on commercial vessels from Peru. For example, in the sixteenth century, a black woman sailed from the port of Callao to Valparaíso with her passage costing fifteen pesos plus a hundred-weight of hardtack as food.[6]

It was, nevertheless, the cruel and infamous slave trade either by sea from Peru or overland from Buenos Aires that brought the vast majority of Negroid people to Chile. William F. Sater believes that "many more than 3,000 slaves" entered Santiago by the Peruvian — Pacific route between 1565 and 1615. Philip Curtin estimates that the Atlantic slave trade accounted for the importation of approximately

6,000 persons into Chile during the colonial period. Although Sater, Curtin, and others have proffered only tentative statistics on the slave traffic, there are indications that males far outnumbered females. Until 1640 about two-thirds of the Africans brought to Spanish America were males. In the eighteenth century, the proportion was probably two to one.[7]

The number of free Negroid immigrants to Chile remains unknown. But statistics aside, it is apparent that slave and free women of African ancestry came in substantial numbers. These women together with black, mulata, and zamba children born in the colony constituted a significant segment of the population.

Chapter 1
The Law and Religion

The questions originally raised by Frank Tannenbaum regarding the effect of legal principles, specific legislation, the Church, and religion on the institution of black slavery and race relations in Spanish America have evoked considerable research. While his conclusions have been challenged, and rightly so in many instances,[1] his questions concerning the law and Catholicism are still valid and deserve consideration within the Chilean context.

Legal Status and Legislation

The law regarding slavery rested on the concept that all human beings share a basic spiritual equality and fundamental human rights. Yet the law also reflected a society in which class, race, and color were important. Legislation defined slaves as both persons and property, and because of this duality, specific statutes not only set forth the rights of slaves but also the slave's duties and obligations to the owner and the owner's proprietary authority over the slave. Surely the fact that slavery was hereditary through the maternal line was a tragically bitter aspect of the law for the slave mother who realized that it was through her that her child entered bondage. That principle remained operative until slavery itself was abolished in the nineteenth century. It derived from Roman law as re-stated in the thirteenth-century compilation of Castilian law entitled *Las Siete Partidas,* the most important peninsular legal precedent regarding slavery, the avenues to emancipation, and the lives of manumitted individuals and their descendants.[2]

A sampling of colonial legislation — municipal ordinances, gubernatorial or judicial orders, and royal decrees — that pertained to both free and slave Afro-Chilean women will illustrate the legal regimen. Attention will be given to the legal discrimination that derived from racial or color prejudice as well as social and economic notions. Protective measures that the law extended to Negroid women will also

4

be examined.

A resolution adopted in the city council of Santiago in 1551 stipulated that any Spaniard apprehended after curfew would lose his weapons and face a jail sentence. Male and female blacks and Indians would receive 100 lashes.[3] The basic city ordinances that the cabildo enacted and the audiencia of Lima approved in 1569 also restricted both free black people and slaves. The curfew for black men and women was now set one hour ahead of that for Spaniards. Any black person who was on the streets without a written pass from his or her master would be arrested and lashed. The council passed the ordinance, it said, because black people were committing "many robberies" at night.[4]

The same group of ordinances included three other measures regarding blacks and Indians. (1) The council laid down rules concerning the canals (*acequias*) within Santiago and required anyone who tampered with the waterways to pay for the damage plus a fine of 10 pesos. However, if the guilty party were a black or an Indian, he or she would receive 100 lashes, unless the master wished to prevent the corporal punishment by making the payments established in the ordinance.[5] (2) An ordinance, ostensibly designed to protect Indians, stated that black persons, both free and slave, not only had male and female Indian servants, but many black men had Indian concubines whom they mistreated. Consequently, no black person regardless of his or her "quality or condition" could henceforth have an Indian servant. The penalty was 200 lashes and a fine of 10 pesos payable from any property that the guilty party owned. Owners of black slaves who allowed their slaves to have servants would be fined 50 pesos.[6] (3) A final ordinance accused black people of taking advantage of Indians in business transactions and declared that the only blacks to be allowed in the Indian market in Santiago were those sent to buy commodities for their masters. If they failed to leave promptly after making the purchases, they were subject to 100 lashes.[7]

Racial stereotyping and restrictive legislation with harsh physical punishment were, of course, nothing new in Spanish America and would continue on all legislative levels throughout the colonial period.[8] For example, the licentiate Calderón drafted a set of ordinances for Chile in 1577 that grouped black and mulato slaves together and imposed especially severe penalties on fugitives. Punishment increased according to the number of times a slave escaped and

5

the length of the absence. The maximum penalties for men were castration and death. A slave woman who fled three times or remained a fugitive for over two months would have her breasts removed. It is debatable, however, whether the legislation was ever enforced.[9]

In 1637 the cabildo of Santiago dealt with the question of both Indian and black fugitive slaves. The councilmen at this time were particularly concerned with identifying runaways and preventing householders from harboring or employing them. In order for a comprehensive list of fugitives to be drawn up, owners were to furnish the cabildo notary with the names and descriptions of their absent male and female slaves and note the length of time that each one had been missing. Runaways who were found were to be brought to the authorities or the city jail immediately. Spaniards who concealed or employed fugitives in their homes were subject to a fine of 20 pesos; blacks or Indians would be publicly flogged with 200 lashes. The cabildo records, however, indicate only that the council sought the necessary approval of the ordinance from the audiencia of Santiago, not that the *oidores* (high court judges) granted or denied it.[10]

One reason for the frequent repetition of fugitive slave laws and the harsh penalties that characterized them was the fear of slave rebellions. Black women as well as men came under suspicion of plotting revolt, and in 1658 a black woman was indicted merely for having arrowheads in her possession.[11] Another motive for the fugitive slave laws, however, was the desire to keep slaves at work for their owners.

Slave labor was valued by the Spaniards in Chile, and the cabildo of Santiago more than once went on record in favor of increasing the colony's black population through the slave trade. When a slave trader outlined a proposal to import slaves in 1626, the councilmen declared that the city needed 4,000 black men and women to compensate for the diminished number of Indian workers.[12]

The same concern with the labor question characterized an executive order (*auto*) that Governor Martín de Mujica issued in 1646. He tried to limit the number of male and female black slaves who could be taken from Chile to Peru and was particularly interested in preventing slavers from buying Afro-Chileans with the sole purpose of exporting them. Violators were to be fined 500 pesos for each black person exported in defiance of the auto, and ships' captains who transported the slaves north were threatened with the same penalty.[13]

The king reacted to the gubernatorial measure in a special *cédula* (royal decree) addressed to the audiencia of Santiago on December 13,

THE LAW AND RELIGION

1648. The decree stated that the *fiscal* (crown attorney) of the high court, Juan Huerta Gutiérrez, had reported in a letter dated April 12, 1647, that the governor, on the fiscal's request, had banned the exportation of black slaves to Peru or other places because they were needed as laborers in Chile; now the crown wanted advice from the audiencia before deciding on whether to uphold or revoke the order.[14] Kings and governors notwithstanding, black people continued to be sent to Peru from Chile.[15]

The Spaniards were concerned not only with getting and keeping an adequate labor force in Chile but also with the work capacity of the laborers and regarded alcoholism as a major deterrent to the formation of an upright, industrious working class. Alcoholic addiction was viewed not as a disease but as a cause of sickness, rebellion, crime, and sin among the women and men of all the nonwhite groups. With this assumption, it was logical for Spanish officials to ban the sale of intoxicants to Indians, blacks, and racially mixed castes. The Santiago cabildo accordingly forbade the sale of wine to any non-Spaniards on numerous occasions, especially during the first third of the seventeenth century.[16] Governor Francisco Lazo de la Vega amplified and reenforced the council's temperance campaign in an executive order in 1635.[17]

Some members of the elite that the cabildo represented, nevertheless, undermined these efforts by selling wine from their vineyards to "people of service," including blacks and Indians. Manuel Muñoz de Cuéllar, the fiscal of the audiencia from 1657 to 1663, spoke as a consumer advocate for the poor who were being victimized by the unethical aristocrats and ordinary shopkeepers. He was not adverse to blacks and Indians obtaining wine, but he did object to the sale of the dangerous "new" wine that lacked decoction and caused serious illnesses. It was from this health hazard that he sought to protect the nonwhites. Moreover, the fiscal asserted that all consumers, especially the poor, deserved fair and honest measure when they purchased staples. He consequently favored price controls and inspections to determine that foodstuffs were of good quality. Seven witnesses whom he called to testify before the high court confirmed his views on the abuses perpetrated against consumers within Santiago's territorial jurisdiction and the need for increased regulation of retail sales.[18]

From time to time, the Hapsburg and Bourbon monarchs admonished slave owners in the Indies to provide adequate food and clothing for their slaves. The royal legislation on slave dress sought on the one hand to preserve distinctions of race and class and on the other

7

to enforce principles of modesty.[19] Philip II issued a decree in the first category in 1571 that was incorporated into the *Recopilación de leyes de los reynos de las Indias,* the important seventeenth-century compilation of colonial legislation. The king declared that no black or mulata woman whether she were enslaved or free could wear gold or silver jewelry or silk clothing. However, if she were married to a Spaniard, she could have some of the forbidden jewels and garments made of luxury fabrics.[20]

In 1631 the cabildo of Santiago drew up its own sumptuary legislation. Two of the fourteen ordinances dealt with the dress of Afro-Chileans and Indians. Women from these groups were directed to wear clothing made of common textiles and designed along modest, plain lines without trimming or silk ruffles. If a wealthy white woman went about the city with her female servants, the latter had to observe the dress code or wear a simple, unelaborate livery. Neither men nor women could be accompanied by more than three liveried servants.[21]

There is no evidence that the local sumptuary legislation was enforced, but it prefigured a royal decree that reached Chile later in the seventeenth century because both dealt with the question of modest attire for slave women and sought to upgrade public morality. The decree which the Queen Mother Mariana of Austria signed on December 2, 1672, began, as was customary, with the rationale for the legislation. The regent explained that the Council of the Indies had received reports, "from persons zealous for the service of God," to the effect that black male and female slaves in the Indies were unclothed. It was necessary to remedy this "prejudicial abuse" because "total nudity (especially of women)" constituted an occasion of sin and did not conform to Christian decency and modesty. Therefore, the queen mother ordered the viceroys, presidents of audiencias, and governors throughout the Indies to ensure that black men and women had clothing, "or at least coverings" for modesty's sake so that others could look at them without falling into sin. Each official would be held liable for enforcing this legislation in his *residencia* (judicial review of an official's term of office).[22]

The regent had a practical turn of mind and next outlined steps for the prompt execution and fulfillment of her order. The officials, each in his jurisdictional district, were to have the black men and women appear before them wearing "that type of clothing conducive to natural decency and modesty." If they were free persons and did not dress properly, they would be fined for the first offense; for the second, they would be jailed. For the third, the guilty could be lashed or punished in some other manner befitting the repeated offense. In cases that involved slaves, the owners would have to pay the monetary fines for the first offense. For the second violation, owners would be jailed if it was their fault that the slaves had no clothes. If the slave was at fault, he or she was to be punished in some appropriate way. For the third offense, the slave, if the owner was to blame, would be taken away and either assigned to work in the local hospital or sold and the money given to the hospital.[23]

In the final portion of the decree, the queen mother exhorted the archbishops, bishops, and superiors of religious orders in the Indies to take similar measures regarding the slaves that belonged to churchmen. This, the regent stated, was fitting because such action would prevent "sins against purity and maintain Christian decency," both appropriate concerns of the ecclesiastical authorities. The prelates were also to monitor the civil officials to see that they did not neglect the enforcement of the decree. If it was not observed, reports were to be sent to the crown.[24]

On the same day, the regent issued another cédula aimed at saving black women, free and slave, from being forced into prostitution. This decree, also prompted by informants "zealous for the service of God," applied to Chile and other parts of the Indies. The regent had learned that some owners of slave women required them to spend the daylight hours peddling various commodities; if they returned to their master with insufficient money, they were sent out at night as prostitutes to earn more. Since these reports had shocked the Council of the Indies, it agreed, and the regent now commanded, that the ranking civil officials in their respective districts should "proceed to the punishment of such a scandalous abuse" with due "rigor." To prevent the sins that were "so ugly and unworthy of Christian purity," they were to give the necessary orders and impose the proper penalties. Specifically, they were to require free black women and black slave women to stay in their employers' or owners' houses after nightfall. Municipal officials were to make inspection rounds to see that the orders were carried out. The prelates were urged to use their spiritual and ecclesiastical authority to help remedy the "abomination" and bring about the necessary reform because it was a matter proper to their "pastoral office." Reports on the enforcement proceedings were to be sent to the queen mother.[25]

Although the crown responded to specific complaints regarding dress and prostitution, it ignored the insidious and perhaps more pervasive problem of sexual abuse and exploitation of slave women by their owners. The two seventeenth-century laws nonetheless dealt with serious matters in a serious way. If they were followed at all, they would have the effect of improving the quality of life for women whose hold on human dignity and human rights was always fragile and tenuous.

That the problems of inadequate clothing and prostitution continued into the Bourbon era is demonstrated by a decree dating from 1710 which also condemned the harsh punishments meted out to slaves. The king stated that he was appalled at "the rigorous punishments" some masters inflicted on black people in the Indies. Another "scandalous abuse" was the practice of requiring black and mulata women to earn a daily wage because most of them were sent out unclothed and committed "many mortal sins" in order to accumulate the sums of money their owners demanded. To eliminate such excesses, the king ordered governors and judges to outlaw harsh, cruel punishments; the new moderation should not undermine the slave system, however. The officials were to make sure that slave women were dressed modestly and prohibited from practicing "nudity and unchasteness." If female slaves were found on the streets, they were to be returned to their owners until the reforms were enacted. Prelates were entreated to lend their authority to help prevent scandals and sins.[26]

In spite of their good intentions to spare the slave woman from the degradation of a prostitute's life, both Hapsburgs and Bourbons stopped short of the strict censures which Spain's medieval jurists had imposed on immoral and unethical slave owners who prostituted slaves. The *Siete Partidas* had called for the manumission of any females forced into prostitution by their owners.[27] That far, the latter day monarches were unwilling to go.

The desire to ameliorate abuses and simultaneously perpetuate the institution of slavery is one of the themes running through the royal legislation issued in 1789. This famous "Instruction," the crown's most coherent and comprehensive statement on Negroid slavery, as Charles III himself admitted, contained little that was new and was intended primarily to amplify and clarify existing law which included the *Partidas* and other peninsular legal compilations, the *Recopilación,* and royal decrees. Although the "Instruction" was never fully or evenly enforced, and the crown ordered it suspended in 1794, portions of it were acted upon by the Chilean courts.[28]

For example, in 1793 the audiencia of Santiago ruled that slaves charged with stealing were to be dealt with according to the

"Instruction,"[29] which, in regard to any serious crimes, placed the matter of trial and punishment in the hands of the courts that were to proceed exactly as if the slave were a free person. For minor offenses, the owner or overseer could inflict punishment to a maximum of twenty-five lashes but could neither draw blood nor cause mutilation or serious contusion. No other persons could punish slaves in any fashion. Individuals who violated these provisions were to be tried and sentenced as if the injured person were free. If the owner were the guilty party, the slave could be sold to a new purchaser.[30]

A case heard in 1791 covered several of these points. The mulata slave woman, Nicolasa Mercado, belonged to one man but was flogged on the orders of another who claimed that she had spread rumors about him. The Spaniard who stood accused of mistreating her was nevertheless acquitted in court when it was shown that the flogging did not exceed the twenty-five lashes allowable under the 1789 legislation.[31]

Even under the older laws, slave owners could bring charges when their slaves were arbitrarily mistreated. For example, in 1679 the audiencia of Santiago ordered an inquiry into the conduct of the corregidor of Cuyo. Residents who had complained of his abuse of power included the widow Isabel de Urquiza y Tobar, who alleged that he had flogged one of her black female slaves until it was impossible for the woman to work.[32]

Slaves themselves sometimes gained access to the courts to protest cruel treatment as Rosa de Rojas learned in 1776 when she had to respond to such charges. Her husband's mulata slave, Tadea Aránguiz, maintained that Rosa struck her with her fist and pulled out her hair. Although Tadea presented other slaves to corroborate the evidence, Rosa defended herself with her version of what had transpired, claiming that Tadea's conduct deserved punishment, and eluded censure.[33]

More serious was the case of the young mulata slave, María Nicolasa Márquez, who was included in the dowry for Margarita Márquez when she married Francisco Gómez de la Fraila, a Peruvian. A man of violent temper, Francisco not only had a love affair with María Nicolasa but also beat her. When Margarita heard the rumors of her husband's infidelity, she vented her anger on María Nicolasa who turned to the audiencia for help in 1709. The court ruled that until she could be sold to a new owner she was to be placed in the custody of Catalina Chacón y Carvajal. The two women were attending one of the Holy Week observances, the outdoor procession held at night on

11

Holy Thursday, when Francisco tried to abduct María Nicolasa by force, but one of Catalina's servant women thrust him away. A new owner soon purchased María Nicolasa for 800 pesos and probably took her to Concepción, a safe distance from her former molester. Meanwhile, Catalina sued Francisco for his insulting behavior. He was punished with a jail sentence and at least a temporary embargo on his property.[34]

The seventeenth-century court proceedings against the sadistic *encomendera*-slave owner, Catalina de los Ríos, still await a thorough re-examination in the tribunal of history. For example, the precise composition of the audiencia bench at the several stages of the inquiries, hearings, convictions, sentences, and appeals should be set forth in full detail. Equally important is the need to unravel the various factional disputes within the high court that were contemporaneous with her cases. This research is necessary to test the validity of the allegations that judicial partiality shielded "La Quintrala" from full punishment for her crimes. The charges against her, on the other hand, have already received considerable attention. Some audiencia ministers, working to hold her accountable for her atrocities, compiled and studied testimony from witnesses including Indians and Afro-Chileans. The evidence shows that she was guilty of the rather common abuses of failing to furnish adequate clothing for her nonwhite servants and slaves, neglecting her responsibility to provide them with religious instructions and services, keeping some married couples apart, and forcing other men and women into marriage. The court records further reveal that her servitors were flogged until the blood ran and then suffered the excruciating pain of having urine, salt, or pepper rubbed into the wounds. Burns were inflicted also. These tortures resulted in the death of some forty victims: male and female Afro-Chileans, Indians, and at least one Spanish girl.[35]

Catalina de los Ríos, the criminal slave owner, was the worst but not the only perpetrator of cruel and unusual punishment. For example, evidence of torturing the mulata slave, María de los Angeles, appeared in a case in 1795 concerning thefts from her owner Agustín Argüelles by one José González and his accomplices. Agustín admitted in court that he had beaten her, confined her in fetters, and made her dress in sackcloth in order to force her to inform on those who committed the robberies. The audiencia of Santiago ruled that he must be more moderate when punishing his slaves in the future and not exceed the twenty-five lashes that the royal law of 1789 stipulated. If additional punishment were required, he must turn the matter over to the courts.

María de los Angeles, then twenty years of age, was sentenced to be sold away from Santiago. She could not return to the city for a period of six years under threat of being sent to Juan Fernández Island as a settler. An outsider was instructed to assess her value and take into account that she was a thief and a runaway. When her price was set at 225 pesos, her disgruntled owner objected that it was too low.[36]

The complaint about the price was typical of cases concerning letters of sale (*cartas,* or *papeles, de venta*). According to the *Partidas,* the slave who sought release from a cruel owner could obtain such a document. If slave and owner failed to agree on a price, the courts could intervene.[37] In two eighteenth-century cases, slave women named María del Carmen Gutiérrez and Candelaria obtained letters of sale from their respective female owners, María Mercedes de los Ríos and María Lozano. In each document, the owner listed the slave's accomplishments and talents in order to receive a higher price. Because of her youth, good health, and skills in sewing, cooking, washing, and ironing, María del Carmen was priced at 500 pesos. Although Candelaria argued that she was more than 60 years old and ill, her owner insisted on a price of 200 pesos because she was a cook as well as laundress.[38]

Slaves frequently sought letters of sale in Chile in order to avoid being sold away to Peru. Rosa Villalón, a slave woman born in Africa, argued eloquently in 1757 that she should not be sold outside of Chile because she considered it her "own fatherland" and her parents lived there. To be sent to Peru would constitute an act of cruelty and condemn her "to a civil death and to a perpetual exile." Her owner had given her a letter of sale but set the price at 450 pesos. Although she asked that the price be lowered to 350 in order to find a purchaser in Chile, the court refused, and her owner had his way.[39]

In the eighteenth century, Chilean slaves who took their owners to court were represented by a public defender who occasionally won his case.[40] Ironically, in suits concerning letters of sale, the slave and his or her attorney had to demean the person's worth in order to make it easier to find a new owner at a lower price. On the other hand, the legal principle of redress against a cruel owner demonstrates that a slave owner's property rights were not absolute.

A special category of law, derived from peninsular legislation, countenanced several avenues to freedom. Through their wills, Chilean slave owners could and did translate their gratitude for faithful service into manumission. Some slave owners, no doubt, used a deathbed bequest of liberty as a form of restitution for wrong-doing to ease a guilty conscience.

Clauses that manumitted slaves could, however, be annulled by the courts if the testator's debts exceeded his or her assets. In other instances, heirs disputed the validity of testamentary manumissions. Wills might also retract earlier manumissions. A particularly involved case concerned María del Tránsito whose owner had liberated her and her seven children in 1774 only to annul their emancipation in his will a quarter of a century later. His heirs sued to retain ownership of the children and, while they had control of them, sold them to outsiders. It took five years in court, but María del Tránsito and her children were able to use the original manumission document that contained a nonrevokable clause to obtain a ruling restoring their liberty.[41]

Wills themselves could call for conditional or delayed manumission or leave the question of freedom to the executors or heirs.[42] For example, Governor Rodrigo de Quiroga left a directive regarding his wish to manumit a slave woman worth fifty ducats who had worked for him for thirty years. In 1590 his grandson-in-law, Antonio de Quiroga, grumbled about the financial obligation this had imposed on him and on his deceased wife, the governor's granddaughter and heiress, Inés de Quiroga y Gamboa.[43]

Delayed manumissions figured in two eighteenth-century testaments. (1) A woman who wrote her will in 1757 declared that her widower was to retain her slave María Josefa for fourteen years and then release her from bondage.[44] (2) The testamentary dispositions of María Hidalgo, the widow of the notary Juan Bautista de Borda, were somewhat similar. In her will of July 6, 1786, María stated that her grandson Tadeo de Reyes had already obtained three slaves: the black woman Bernarda, presumably the same person mentioned later in regard to Inés de Borda Hidalgo's estate; Bernarda's young mulato son, Manuel; and another mulato named José Bernardo. On February 8, 1787, María authorized a codicil in which she declared that her slave Javiera Borda and the woman's daughter, Rosa, should be given their freedom; however, Rosa was to work for Tadeo until she married or reached the age of twenty-five.[45]

A third will dating from the eighteenth century featured a special kind of delayed, conditional manumission. María Constanza Marín de Poveda y Azúa, an encomendera who would inherit the marquisate of Cañada Hermosa in 1772, acknowledged an obligation to free two slaves her deceased husband had owned. With his power of attorney, she wrote his posthumous will on December 17, 1757, and stated that she was to manumit any two of the male or female slaves within eight years. According to his instructions, she could elect the persons who served her most faithfully and seemed least likely to dissipate their liberty.[46] Human freedom, regarded as a privilege rather than an inherent right, was held out as a reward for good conduct. The many slaves could be encouraged to work harder and better when an owner promised liberty to a few.

As will be seen, José de Toro Zambrano, the bishop of Concepción, declined to liberate his sister's slaves, Floriana and María Isabel, because he thought they would have more security if they remained as bondswomen. Since some slave owners refused to support elderly or sick slaves and granted manumission only when those persons were unable to care for themselves, the crown legislated against that abuse in the "Instruction" of 1789.[47]

It was possible to purchase freedom from a slave owner. The slave, another individual, or an organization such as a *cofradía* (religious confraternity and mutual aid society) could present the purchase price to the owner in order to obtain manumission. Royal law spoke in favor of allowing a father, who was free, to purchase the liberty of his offspring born of a slave mother,[48] and two Chilean cases of this type have been discovered.

In 1770 Toribio Villegas purchased his daughter's freedom from her owner Josefa Díaz de Guzmán for 150 pesos. The mulata child, Luisa Villegas, was 4 years old at the time.[49]

In the seventeenth century, Andrea, a mulata between seven and eight years old, obtained her freedom as the result of a pact between her father and her owner. Andrea and her mother Elena belonged to the widow Elena de la Serna. The child was released from slavery for two reasons. In the first place, her father, Juan Flamenco, deeded her owner his Angolan slave of the same age named Lucrecia. Secondly, Elena de la Serna wanted to reward "the services" Andrea's mother had done for her. The full irony of the situation is brought home by the manumission document dated February 23, 1623, in which Elena de la Serna stated that she gave Andrea "liberty," and Juan Flamenco defined young Lucrecia as a "slave and subject to perpetual servitude."[50] The price of one child's freedom was the continued enslavement of another.

An eighteenth-century case with a sad beginning had a happy ending. A mulato slave named Vicente borrowed 150 pesos from a Spaniard to purchase his freedom. As collateral for repayment of the loan, he pledged his free-born daughter, María, whose mother was a free Indian woman. Vicente's creditor then ceded María to another Spaniard for whom she worked for several years. When she sued for release from this form of bondage, the audiencia ruled in 1720 that she was free and ordered each Spaniard to pay her 75 pesos as compensation for her labor. The man for whom she had worked was required to pay the 150 pesos Vicente had borrowed, and the notary who had witnessed the original transaction was fined 50 pesos.[51] At the dawn of the age of the Enlightenment, the audiencia of Santiago frowned on the practice of pawning free persons and condemning them to servitude. Peninsular legislation was, nevertheless, contradictory on such practices. *Las Siete Partidas,* modeled on Roman law which allowed men to enslave their children, permitted a father, but not a mother, to sell or pawn minor-age children as a last resort to save the family from starvation. The older, seventh-century *Visigothic Code* strictly prohibited parents from selling their children, giving them away, or using them as surety for payment of debts.[52] Regardless of whether the Chilean high court consciously or unconsciously upheld the Visigothic law, María regained her freedom and obtained some funds to start a new life.

A thorough search of archival materials would no doubt produce additional information on the women manumitted in Spanish Chile. But how many female slaves heard a promise of liberation or saved money toward a future self-purchase and never reached the desired goal cannot be known.

If manumission liberated a person from the dehumanizing condition of bondage, it did not eradicate racial and social bias. Racial slurs are common in contemporary records. Local documents as well as royal legislation demonstrate widespread bigotry toward free men and women of African ancestry. At the same time, individual Afro-Chilean women were recognized for their personal worth.

The contradictory phenomena appear in juxtaposition in Chilean court cases arising from eighteenth-century royal decrees seeking to discourage "unequal" marriages. In audiencia cases, suitors and prospective brides were alleged to be socially unacceptable on the grounds of race or lowly occupation and, sometimes, illegitimacy. While a white parent, abetted by the legislation, might use the civil courts to try to prevent a child from marrying a Negroid person, the fact of interracial marriage indicates that prejudice was not universal among young people seeking marital partners.[53]

Religion and the Church

Marriage was defined by the Church as a sacrament regardless of the status or race of the contracting parties; the State, on the other hand, exercised jurisdiction over the civil aspects of the marital bond. The interaction of the two authorities on marriage questions was typical of many matters influencing the lives of Afro-Chileans.

Both Church and State accepted responsibility for the spiritual welfare of Afro-Chileans. Royal legislation insisted upon the conversion of slaves to Christianity and stressed that slave owners had to provide opportunities for slaves to attend religious instructions and services. Governors and audiencias bore an obligation to see that owners not only refrained from cruel, excessive punishments but also met their slaves' spiritual as well as temporal needs.[54] The crown, as already mentioned, routinely called upon the ecclesiastical authorities for help with questions involving the rights of slaves and public morality. The Church on its own initiative worked for the evangelization of Negroid women and provided them with opportunities and even stringent commands to practice the faith.[55]

Alonso de Ovalle, the famous seventeenth-century Jesuit chronicler, is often cited as an example of a creole priest who worked among the Afro-Chileans in Santiago and was instrumental in organizing one of the cofradías that played an important role in the religious and socio-economic life of the city.[56] Besides participating in Sunday services, religious processions, and the colorful pageantry of Holy Week, this Negroid confraternity, which included both male and female members, performed numerous works of charity such as visiting the city jail, comforting the inmates, providing them with an annual free meal, praying with those sentenced to death, and accompanying the condemned to the place of execution in order to strengthen their spirit in "that last critical moment."[57]

Of special concern to Ovalle and his fellow Jesuits were the *bozales* (African-born blacks) recently arrived in Chile via Buenos Aires or Peru. Ovalle's description of them makes grim reading. The bozales, he noted, were of such limited intelligence that they seemed to be brute beasts rather than men. Furthermore, they emitted a "bad odor" which was particularly offensive when they fell ill. (Given the filthy conditions in which the bozales were forced to live, this was not surprising). This unpleasant fact had its compensation, however, in spiritual coin, Ovalle observed. The catechist and the confessor who ministered to these unfortunate wretches had ample opportunity to store up merit in heaven through the exercise of charity, patience, and self-mortification in caring for their spiritual needs. Occasionally he even witnessed the gratifying effects of his work as Ovalle himself did in the case of a black slave woman who was critically ill. After a long, seemingly fruitless effort to instruct her, she grasped the rudiments of the faith, received conditional baptism, and died.[58] Ovalle cited such instances as proof that "with time and patience" and "the efficacy of divine grace" the bozales could be converted to Christianity.[59]

To conclude from the disparaging remarks about bozales that Ovalle was a racist would be unwarranted, especially since he emphasized that, despite their poverty and ignorance, they were capable of acquiring knowledge and of frequenting the sacraments. His further contention that Chilean-born blacks and *ladinos* (hispanized Negroids) had as much mental ability as Spaniards suggests that a lack of acculturation rather than race was the reason for his criticism.[60] Similarly, the story of the slave woman's deathbed conversion served to underline his conviction regarding the intellectual ability of bozales to comprehend complex doctrinal truths even in such extreme circumstances.

Despite the selfless efforts of men like Ovalle, the institution of Negroid slavery had become so ingrained in the Spanish American colonies that it was common for individual ecclesiastics and religious orders — female and male, including the Society of Jesus — to own slaves. Rodrigo González Marmolejo, the first bishop of Santiago, had a black female servant who was probably a slave but, in spite of this, the woman held title to a city lot in 1558. In the eighteenth century, Bishop Toro Zambrano also owned slaves.[61]

The Spanish value system nevertheless expected clerics to be in the front line of defense of human rights, including the right to marry freely. Given that premise, it was logical for priests to be held accountable in this regard. One such instance involved Rodrigo González Marmolejo, before he became a bishop, and Catalina de Mella, a mulata servant of Inés Suárez. An investigation into his private and priestly life in 1556 alleged that he had misused his spiritual authority in blessing a marriage, Catalina's third, to Bernardino de Mella while a previous husband was still living. Testimony on the charge indicated that she had been coerced into her first marriage as a very young child of only eight or nine years.[62]

Although Inés Suárez was not held responsible for any aspect of the marriages, Bernardino de Mella had a very low opinion of the famous *conquistadora* (female conqueror).[63]

Two hundred years later, the Bishop of Santiago, Manuel de Alday, was concerning himself with safeguarding slave marriages. In 1757 he and Governor Amat y Junient tried to discourage the forcible separation of married couples and imposed restrictions on slavers who transported Afro-Chileans to Peru.[64] Churchmen of the diocese of Santiago, meeting in the Synod of 1763 under the direction of the same prelate, sought to restrain owners from selling married slaves to different buyers.[65] An earlier synod held in 1688 had defended the right of slaves to marry freely.[66] Although these efforts addressed the principle of the sanctity of matrimony, neither ecclesiastical nor civil legislation could fully protect slave marriages and families from unconscionable owners and slavers.

No analysis of the impact of Church and State on the lives of Negroid persons would be complete without mention of that most controversial politico-ecclesiastical institution, the Holy Office of the Inquisition. Over the centuries, the Holy Office, charged with defending morality and preserving doctrinal orthodoxy, heard cases that involved Afro-Chilean women. In the earliest one, dating from 1587, a free black woman named Inés was charged with bigamy but apparently was acquitted. In 1725 in Lima, the branch of the Inquisition that exercised jurisdiction over Chileans found a domestic servant named María Zapata, a free zamba, guilty of the same offense. Her sentence included a flogging.[67]

Juana de Castañeda, a zamba born in Valdivia, was living in the Peruvian port town of Callao at the turn of the sixteenth century when, at the age of thirty-two, the Inquisition accused her of various practices that were deemed superstitious. A chief witness against her was a mulata woman on whom she had allegedly inflicted a knife wound. Juana was sentenced to 100 lashes and exiled from Callao for 2 years.[68]

A zamba slave from Santiago, María de Silva, a cook and a married woman, who was also known by the name Marota de Cuadros, was fifty years old when the Lima Inquisition indicted her. She was charged specifically with telling fortunes for female clients. Found guilty in 1737, she was sentenced to spiritual penances, 200 lashes, a monetary fine, and exile to the southern fort of Valdivia for 10 years.[69]

As Leslie B. Rout, Jr. has observed, Negroids brought before the

Inquisition "could expect neither tolerance nor compassion." These cases, dating from the sixteenth through the eighteenth centuries, indicate that he is equally correct in noting that time did not soften the severity of Inquisition sentences.[70]

In spite of some benefits and protections put forth by Church and State, religion and the law, the social and political milieu of the Afro-Chilean woman remained harsh, restrictive, and even barbarous. How she surmounted these impediments and made meaningful contributions to the colonial economy is discussed in the next chapter.

Chapter 2
The Economy

Afro-Chilean women counted in the economy in two basic ways. In the first place, the monetary value of slaves represented capital assets in private fortunes. The importation of slaves, the internal slave trade, and slave ownership all figured in the Chilean economy and emphasized the proprietary nature of slavery. The law which recognized slaves as persons also held that slaves were property that could be bought and sold, used as a substitute for money in almost any type of transaction, and as surety for the payment of debts. Slaves could be given in dowries and incorporated in *mayorazgos* (entailed estates).[1] Secondly, through working and acquiring property, Afro-Chilean women played active economic roles thus demonstrating their initiative as individuals and their legal capacity as persons.

The Slave Trade

The traffic in human beings represented a source of income for both large-scale slave traders and individuals who obtained licenses to import small numbers of slaves with the intent to sell them in Chile. Since much slaving activity was in the form of illegal smuggling, it is doubtful that a full tally of the persons who engaged in the trade and those who were its subjects will ever be forthcoming.[2] Given the inadequacy of the data, a few illustrations to supplement those mentioned previously will have to suffice.

Francisco García de Huidobro, a Castilian immigrant, imported a number of blacks from Buenos Aires during the 1730s and reputedly received 20,000 pesos when he sold the men and women in Chile and Peru. Later in life, this slave trader paid an identical sum for a title of nobility that commemorated his foundation and operation of the royal mint in Santiago.[3]

FORGOTTEN FEMALES

A prominent seventeenth-century merchant and bureaucrat, Alonso del Campo Lantadilla, the proprietary *alguacil mayor* (chief constable) and alderman in the city of Santiago, also engaged in the slave trade.[4] Moreover, the dowry he provided for his illegitimate daughter, Magdalena del Campo Lantadilla, included funds which her husband, Juan Cajal, invested in a slave trade venture. Juan furnished capital in the form of 3,300 silver pesos, that he had just received in the second installment of the dowry, and 277 gold pesos, the monetary value of a gold chain. His business agent, Fernando Bravo de Naveda, agreed to travel to Buenos Aires where he would purchase at least four black females and as many young adult males as the funds would allow, with the understanding that approximately twenty-eight pesos each would be required for providing the slaves with food and clothing and transporting them to Chile. As compensation, Fernando was to receive one-fourth of the eventual profits. If the Buenos Aires slave market had no human chattels, he would use the money to purchase merchandise as Juan directed in a memorandum. The contract preserved in the registry of the notary Manuel de Toro Mazote bears the signatures of the business associates and states that the chief constable witnessed the document.[5]

Further archival material from the same registry provides data on the Chilean internal slave trade and the African origins of women. In the four-month period extending from November 5, 1622, to February 25, 1623, Toro Mazote listed transactions in Santiago involving sixteen female slaves, thirteen of whom were from Angola; ten were described as "recently come" from their homelands. The owner of a forty-year-old mulata from Lisbon exchanged the woman for fifty pesos plus the eighteen-year-old Angolan, Gracia, who was suffering from an illness. The teenagers, Cristina and Juliana, were sold with the Angolan males, Anton and Diego, for a total of 1,810 pesos. Aldonza de Guzmán purchased Lucrecia, a woman 25 years of age, and Luisa, 17 years old, for 900 pesos payable to the chief constable Alonso del Campo Lantadilla within 6 months during which time he retained a lien on the slaves. Inés, 16 years old, and María, estimated to be between 18 and 20 years of age, commanded the slightly higher price of 920 pesos from a man acting for Mariana de Villagra, who had 8 months to make the final payment. The Angolan mother, Lucrecia, approximately 50 years old, and her young children, Ana and Domingo, respectively 4 and 5 years of age, were purchased by Catalina Justiniano for 600 pesos. Only 4 females, each named María, were sold individually. The youngest of these, aged 12, and an Angolan, aged 18, brought a price of 300 pesos each, while those who were 17 and 20 years old, cost 440 and 450 pesos, respectively. As already mentioned, the owner of Lucrecia, a little girl from Angola, used her in an agreement with Elena de la Serna to obtain freedom for his mulata daughter, Andrea.[6] These bills of sale and exchange with their poignant descriptions of the persons sold and bartered indicate that further examination of notarial records will yield much more than cold, quantitative data for a study of the slave trade.

These manuscript sources and published documents on slave sales followed a standard form. Each bill of sale emphasized that the seller had clear title to the slave and transferred ownership to the buyer in exchange for an agreed upon price. The age, characteristics, distinguishing features, appearance, and health of the slave were explained in general or specific terms. For example, it was common for bozales to be described as frightened and malnourished to the point of being mere skin and bones. In selling women and girls newly brought from Africa, the documents routinely noted that the slaves had been acquired in a "just war" and were subject to captivity.[7] The typical bill of sale obviously treated the slave as a vendible commodity or piece of merchandise.

Slave Ownership

Once a sale agreement had been concluded, the slave belonged to the purchaser and could be retained, manumitted, or relinquished to another owner. The profit motive no doubt goes far to explain why relatively few slaves were set free. Parents did nonetheless give slaves to their children, particularly in dowries. A slave was not only a status symbol and a financial asset but, in the case of household staff, might also act as confidant and companion as well as servant to the new bride. The several roles expected of a bondswoman working as a maid did not, however, alter the fact that she was property.

The most highly touted seventeenth-century dowry promised to entail real estate in favor of María de Torres y Olivares, the fiancée of Cristóbal Mesía y Valenzuela. In addition to the mayorazgo, the first in Chile, the formal marital endowment written in 1686 listed twelve slaves, including four black females and two young mulatas. The two youngest slaves were seven-year-old girls and the oldest was a woman forty-five years of age. The monetary evaluations of the women and

girls were as follows:
  A black married woman, Ana, 40 years old, worth 600 pesos.
  A black woman, Antonia, 45 years old, worth 450 pesos.
  A mulata, Sebastiana, 12 years old, worth 400 pesos.
  A black child, Tomasa, 11 years old, worth 400 pesos.
  A mulata child, Josefa, 7 years old, worth 250 pesos.
  A black child, María Ejipciaca, 7 years old, worth 250 pesos.
The prices totaled 2,350 pesos and, with the value of the male slaves, comprised 5,750 pesos of the projected, ostensible total dowry of 100,000 pesos.[8] Expressed as percentages, the female slaves constituted 2.4, the males 3.4, and together the men, women, and children 5.8 percent of the marital endowment.

A smaller and more typical dowry, dating from earlier in the seventeenth century, included 5 slaves whose combined worth was 1,830 pesos. The notary's memorandum on the property gave the following itemized appraisals of the slaves:
  A black Angolan, Juan, 18 years, worth 450 pesos.
  A *ladina,* Isabel, a maker of conserves, 29 years, worth 650 pesos.
  A mulato, Pedro, 14 years, worth 330 pesos.
  A mulata, Jusepa, 10 years old, worth 250 pesos.
  A younger mulata, Petrona, worth 150 pesos.
The rest of the endowment consisted of household goods, a trousseau, silverware, and jewelry to raise the total to 4,083 pesos. The bridegroom furnished an *arras* (wedding gift to the bride) of 1,000 pesos. The document pertained to the dowry consigned to Pedro de Astorga who entered a marriage contract with Inés de Molina on March 24, 1635.[9] The slaves entrusted to him thus comprised 36 percent of the bride's total estate consisting of the dowry and arras. The female slaves represented 20.7 percent of Inés de Molina's financial assets at the time of marriage.

Eighteenth-century women who obtained slaves as gifts or dowry bonuses included two daughters of Manuel Calvo de Encalada y Chacón, the second marqués de Villapalma. He and his wife, Margarita Recabarren Pardo de Figueroa, endowed their daughter, María Teresa, with 26,000 pesos. Manuel noted in his will that he had given María Teresa the slave, Petronila, and items of clothing; neither the slave nor the trousseau were to be deducted from her paternal inheritance. After Margarita Recabarren died, the marqués provided a dowry of 16,500 pesos for their daughter María Antonia. Manuel also gave her a gold reliquary with pearls and diamonds that had been her mother's and a slave named Teresa. According to his will, the slave woman and the reliquary were hers to keep above and beyond her necessary parental inheritance.[10] His concern was not with the slaves as persons. Rather, when his estate would be divided, he wanted his daughters to remain in undisputed possession of the slaves Petronila and Teresa without sharing their monetary value with the other heirs.

The posthumous estate settlement of the young matron, Inés de Borda Hidalgo, in 1763 records data on slaves in the same matter-of-fact tone used in regard to material objects. Of the four slaves mentioned in the proceedings, two were females. An appraiser assigned the value of 250 pesos to a mulata slave, Petronila, approximately 40 years old. She was routinely designated as part of the community property that Inés and her widower and second husband, José Alberto Díaz, had acquired. José Alberto, at one point, sought to establish that the other female slave, Bernarda, a black teenager, also belonged to the Díaz y Borda conjugal estate. He relinquished the claim, however, when his in-laws, Juan Bautista de Borda and María Hidalgo, denied that they had given Bernarda to their deceased daughter, Inés.[11]

One of the most distinguished seventeenth-century widows, Isabel Osorio de Cáceres, displayed a slightly less callous, if nonetheless proprietary, attitude toward her black slaves. Isabel, the eldest child of a conquistador and his peninsular wife, was the daughter-in-law of an ex-governor of Chile. During her widowhood, she administered a large encomienda entrusted to her son, Diego Bravo de Saravia, and owned both urban and rural real estate. In her last will and testament, this matriarch of a family that later rose to noble status mentioned her slaves. Isabel listed the Christian names, but not the occupations, of ten slaves: five men and five women. The posthumous inventory, however, identified only nine slaves, including three married couples. Despite her considerable assets, Isabel was not untypical of the debt-ridden elite, and perhaps her financial liabilities explain why she did not choose to manumit any of her Afro-Chilean slaves. In any event, her only compensation or restitution to them was the bequest of two pieces of grogram clothing each.[12]

Seventeenth-century documents pertaining to Lorenza Bernal de Mercado and her poet-historian husband, Juan de Mendoza Monteagudo,[13] reveal several facets of chattel slavery. Lorenza and Juan were gravely ill in Santiago on November 16, 1666, when they each issued a power of attorney for the Jesuit priest, Fernando de Mendoza, and Antonio de Zárate y Bello to write their will and named the latter, whom Juan identified as his nephew, as custodian of their posthumous estate. Juan also prepared two memoranda to guide the testators who utilized all the papers in the decedents' joint will dated February 25, 1667. On March 6 the nephew inventoried the estate. These private records mention six slaves. [14]

Since Lorenza and Juan had neither surviving ascendants nor legitimate children, they both designated his four natural daughters as their heiresses; Juan also recognized five natural sons and set aside a small bequest of one hundred pesos for three of them to share. [15]

Lorenza's power of attorney contained only one personal bequest: a directive for her mulato slave, Alonso, to be manumitted so that "as a free person" he could execute "contracts, wills, and documents," and undertake other legal activities. [16] Juan approved the emancipation and declared that Alonso was believed to be the son of his first cousin, Pedro de Escobar. The posthumous will declared Alonso free, and the inventory noted that he had actually received his liberty. [17]

For reasons of kinship, Alonso had been released from bondage. Five female slaves, however, remained in slavery. For example, Juan had acted as the executor of the estate of his deceased sister, María de Mendoza. Since it was still not entirely settled, he instructed his own executors to assume his duties and explained that one of María's slave women had been seized for debt. To recover the mulata, Juan had borrowed thirty pesos from one María de Riberos, who was now to be repaid. [18]

The testamentary dispositions and posthumous inventory also discussed the past and present fate of four other female slaves. Juan had sold a black teenager named Petrona with the stipulation that he could regain her if he repaid the selling price. This he evidently had not done, because Petrona was still in the purchaser's possession at the time of the inventory. Juan had placed the youngest slave, Catalina, who was 12 years old, in the care of a niece who had loaned him approximately 200 pesos. She was supposed to teach the black child "to serve" in return for her work; however, Juan stated in a memo that Catalina might have to be sold to meet expenses for his funeral or that of his wife. Should this occur, the niece could buy Catalina and deduct the previous loan from the price of the slave, or one of his daughters might pay the niece. The inventory is not entirely clear about Catalina's status, but apparently she became the property of the niece. This would mean that the only slave still pertaining to the posthumous estate was Francisca, a mulata who was twenty-two years of age, because, long ago, Juan and Lorenza had given their mulata slave María, now between eighteen and twenty years old, to his natural

26

daughter, Jerónima de la Mota, as partial compensation for her help in the household.[19]

As the following example shows, males as well as females received slaves from their parents. The case concerns descendants of Isabel Osorio de Cáceres. In 1728 the Marquesa de la Pica, Marcela Norberta Bravo de Saravia Iturrisara, and the Marqués consort, Antonio de Irarrázaval y Bravo de Saravia, provided their son, Miguel, with two slaves. His parents were anticipating his necessary parental inheritance by turning over to him property worth 19,789 pesos 2 reales. The slaves — a bozal youth named Louis, who was valued at 320 pesos, and a woman named Agustina, between 46 and 48 years of age, and priced at only 250 pesos because of illness — represented 2.9 percent of the total. While household furnishings and luxury articles were described and separately appraised, most of the property consisted of livestock and tools located on the Bravo estancias.[20] The rural land and the family residence were entailed in Miguel's favor once he had received the slaves, livestock, and movable goods.[21]

An entail founded in 1744 by Juan Nicolás de Aguirre and his first wife, Ignacia Díaz Aséndegui, called for nine slaves to be an inalienable part of the mayorazgo. If any of the eight black males died, new slaves were to be purchased as replacements, but nothing specific was said regarding the replacement of the black woman. The document of foundation stipulated that a percentage of the mayorazgo income might in future be used to purchase more black slaves, "some of whom [should be] married," because their work would augment the value of the estate. The founders thus fully realized the importance of black labor in building private fortunes and tacitly acknowledged the economic contributions that Afro-Chileans made to the colony at large. Yet at the same time, they followed the usual procedure of banning the heirs to the entail from marrying any parties except whites of unquestionable religious orthodoxy. The mayorazgo belatedly took effect but for extraneous reasons did not include any slaves.[22]

The Condes de la Conquista, Mateo de Toro Zambrano and Nicolasa Valdés y Carrera, actually incorporated two female slaves, appraised together at 700 pesos, in the mayorazgo they established in 1789. Predictably, no beneficiary of the estate could choose a marriage partner of full or partial African ancestry. Special injunctions ordered masses to be said on a regular basis both in Santiago and on the entailed estancia for the souls of the founders and all those to whom they were obligated in "justice and charity." The priest who offered the masses at the estancia was also to instruct the domestic servants in

Christian doctrine. Each week the heir had to give the urban poor in Santiago 150 loaves of bread or donate its equivalent to the poorhouse.[23]

The same family gave further evidence of the aristocratic attitude that, on the one hand, regarded slaves as property and, on the other, sought to help the downtrodden. For example, when Nicolasa Valdés made her will in 1810, she still owned a number of slaves, some of whom she manumitted. The remaining slaves were to elect their new owners from among her daughters.[24]

Earlier, the condes had enhanced their daughters' marital dowries with slaves. For example, they endowed their daughter Mercedes with 26,500 pesos in 1781 for her marriage to the superintendent of the royal mint. Since the mulato slave, Miguel, was added to the dowry as a free gift, his value was not computed in the monetary total. At the time of her birth in 1759, one of the Toro Zambrano brides had been promised a young mulata as a personal maid by Mateo's godfather and relative, Bishop José de Toro Zambrano. The bishop's sister, Francisca de Paula de Toro Zambrano, had died in Santiago the previous year and bequeathed her slaves to him. She left to his discretion the manumission of the mulata, Floriana, and the black woman María Isabel, who had shown her their love and fidelity. In a letter to Mateo, the bishop explained that he thought it inadvisable to grant the women liberty because no one would care for them, provide them with medical care, or even see to their eventual burial. As freedwomen they would face "a thousand hardships" without anyone to protect them. He accordingly preferred that Mateo take charge of all the servants in the decedent's home. Nicolasa was to see to it that Floriana and María Isabel received some cloth as a sign of appreciation for their faithful service. Floriana's two sons were to be assigned to Mateo's small boys and in due course accompany them to school as pages.[25]

Occupations

If the slave woman was a capital asset and status symbol for upper class Chileans, who rewarded her more often with tokens of compensation and compassion than with freedom, she was also a direct contributor to the colonial economy. Afro-Chilean women, free and slave, shared the female world of work with poor whites, Indians, and mestizas.

THE ECONOMY

Many or most of the Afro-Chilean women were employed in domestic work, but, in that day before industrialization had brought labor saving devices and manufactured articles into the home, this encompassed a wide range of occupations and a variety of skills. Afro-Chilean, Spanish, Indian, and mestiza women plied their talents to meet those challenges. Cleaning was only one form of "housework." Spinning and weaving were commonplace in early colonial homes. The laundress who could starch and iron was considered more highly skilled than the woman who could only wash clothes. A cook in charge of preparing meals might also have a special talent for making conserves or candies. As the household staff grew in size, the hierarchy of servants became more defined while the number of specialists increased, and an Afro-Chilean woman could become the chief housekeeper with some of the younger girls or women designated as personal maids.[26]

Although the cities had their tailors, there were also seamstresses who made new garments or mended and refashioned old ones for their owners or employers. The work of the seamstress was truly remarkable. To produce the elaborate fashions of the upper class, she had to possess consummate skill as artist, geometrician, and engineer in order to cut, shape, fit, and weld the panels and planes together in a pleasing whole. Merely handling the long, heavy fabrics required stamina. Dexterity was called for in manipulating delicate laces and gossamer textiles shot with metallic threads. A good dressmaker was obviously a prize, but the few documents that mention her wages indicate that her compensation was scant indeed. Like so many anonymous artists through the ages, the colonial seamstress had to be content with low pay, a few compliments, the satisfaction of a job well done, and the joy of creation itself.[27]

Although large homes might have their own ovens for baking bread, most urban residents relied on the bakers in the cities, some of whom were black women.[28] Other Afro-Chilean women engaged in retail sales. Selling fish, a traditional female occupation in Spain, became a matter of concern for the cabildo of Santiago in the seventeenth century. The city council tried to restrict the sale of seafood to a market, and in 1646 auctioned off the franchise for it to the Spaniard, Pedro de Recalde. When he employed an Indian woman, the councilmen complained in June that she did not reserve fish for "privileged persons" as she should and ordered Pedro to hire a Spanish woman. Then in August the council moved against fishmongers who were operating outside the market. Relatively light penalties were imposed for the first and second offense, but any black or Indian woman would be subject to 100 lashes for a third offense while mestizos or Spaniards would be jailed for 10 days.[29]

The city council licensed some of the shops (*pulperías*) that sold wine and foodstuffs in the capital and, as a general rule, preferred to grant the franchises for the shops to Spaniards and wanted whites to work as clerks and barkeeps in them. However, the council repeatedly made exceptions to its own policy and licensed persons from the other ethnic groups to run the pulperías. For example, in 1635 Santiago had twelve pulperías; eight of them were operated by women, one of whom was black and another Indian. Yet in 1631, the cabildo, without explaining why, had denied a franchise to the free black woman, María de Quiñones, who applied for one.[30]

By the early eighteenth century the city councils of Santiago and La Serena customarily conceded pulpería licenses to upper class Hispanic widows.[31] Later in the century, the Santiago councilmen complained to Governor Antonio Guill y Gonzaga that wine shops, now run by men and women of the lower classes also, had become fronts for prostitution and other illegal activities. The governor responded with an executive order in 1763 regulating the shops and stipulating that all women who wanted to run them had to have written licenses from the municipal authorities.[32]

The data on the retail outlets thus reveal prejudice and job discrimination. Individual women did, however, become shopkeepers as well as clerks. Further research should be conducted to determine the number and type of employment opportunities in the crafts for the urban working woman.

Because of laws against vagrancy[33] and the need for labor, the poor who could not find jobs were put to work through the contract system in the sixteenth and seventeenth centuries. The historian, Alvaro Jara, has examined the notary documents on contracts authorized by magistrates in Santiago between 1565 and 1600. During this period, employers hired sixty-one Afro-Chilean men and women. Of this number twenty-three were mulatas and zambas. Only one black woman, a slave named María, appears in the contract lists. In 1597 she agreed to work for a period of four years. As compensation the employer would furnish food and medical care and pay her a salary of twenty-seven and one-half gold pesos. The money would be hers to keep and apply to her purchase of freedom. The data that Jara furnishes do not indicate what type of work María and the other Afro-Chilean women were contracted to perform. Since the amount and form of compensation varied, it is possible that the work did too.[34]

It was not unheard of for slave women to be required to perform manual labor. One such instance was noted in a report drawn up in March, 1654. It noted that some of the black slaves working in a tannery on an estancia were females.[35]

In contrast, some Afro-Chileans were able to become landowners and support themselves in the rural areas. In 1588 a free mulato named Pedro Ponce and his wife, identified only as Catalina, purchased a small plot of land, located some three leagues from Santiago, from two Indian *caciques* (headmen). As payment they gave each Indian headman a garment, one of which was a green dress trimmed with crimson silk edging for the wife of the cacique, Don Juan. The sale, supervised by the administrator of the Indian village and the local priest, vested full title to the land in the married couple and their heirs. Their daughter, Ana Ponce, produced the bill of sale on March 6, 1604, as proof that she and her brother had inherited the property. This occurred during the early seventeenth-century land survey conducted in the Central Valley that involved not only measuring acreage, placing landmarks, and defining boundary lines but also verifying land titles. The surveyor honored the land deed that Ana Ponce presented and noted that the property included a residence and a furnace or an oven.[36]

On rare occasions, an Afro-Chilean woman had the opportunity to acquire a fortune. The colonial historian, Diego de Rosales, told of a black woman who staked a claim in the placer mines near the southern city of Valdivia in the sixteenth century and obtained gold worth 900 pesos from her rich strike.[37]

Such wealth quickly won could be as quickly lost, especially on the Araucanian frontier, and few women could expect such a windfall. Less exciting, but closer to the deeper drama of life were the health service careers that women from the various racial groups followed. In the seventeenth century, Elena Rolón, the mulata daughter of a Spaniard and the black woman, Elena de Zúñiga, was a midwife in Santiago.[38] Other unnamed women also practiced the healing arts and were called upon from time to time to present their credentials to the city council.[39]

Lives of service were remembered and appreciated. Oral tradition in the Vial family kept alive the way a slave woman had taught Agustín de Vial y Santelices to read, write, and cipher in the eighteenth century. Her grateful pupil went on to become a senator in the national congress after independence and delighted in telling his grandson of

31

his first teacher.[40] Unfortunately, the historical record is silent on three important counts. It fails to report how the Afro-Chilean acquired the knowledge that she transmitted to the child in an age that offered few educational opportunities to females of any race and class. Neither does it disclose the woman's personal assessment of her life in bondage. Nor does it reveal whether or not this educated woman obtained her liberty.

Final abolition of the institution of Negroid slavery was delayed until after Chile obtained independence from Spain. A series of gradual measures between 1811 and 1833 effected emancipation in the new nation.[41] Until that time, the experience of Afro-Chilean women remained a mix of cruelty, exploitation, and repression with ameliorative features, never fully compensating for the injustices perpetrated but sometimes making a difference in the quality of life. Through no fault of their own, the harsh system crushed many women; others not only resisted it but survived with courage and dignity, helping to build the colony.

PART II
INDIAS AND MESTIZAS

Castile and, to a lesser extent, Africa provided the basic norms for much of the female activity in Chile, but the Americas too had a living legacy of custom and role definition. Although the Indian world began to change immediately after the arrival of the outsiders, much of Indian culture survived. The traditions of the past continued even as the conquest spread, and, in the unconquered southern frontier areas, the Spanish imprint was scarcely visible when the colony gained its independence in the early nineteenth century. Consequently, the Indian way of life as perceived by men of letters in the colonial period provides insights into the enduring heritage of the indias.

One of the earliest sixteenth-century chroniclers, Gerónimo Bibar, noted Inca influences in the Central Valley. He discussed the Chilean Indians region-by-region, and from Copiapó in the north through the district around Santiago to Concepción and Valdivia in the south, he found a uniform practice of polygamy: the richer and more prestigious the man, the more wives he could buy. In the south, payment to the bride's parents was remitted in sheep, but occasionally the bridegroom supplemented this with clothing or the necklaces made of white bone beads that women wore and prized. The Indians of Valdivia met on an annual basis to settle disputes, conduct the bride sales, and celebrate transactions with drinking parties.[1] Polygamy and consumption of alcohol at celebrations continued to attract comment through the colonial period.[2]

At the beginning of the seventeenth century, the peninsular, Alonso González de Nájera, no friend of the Araucanians, remarked with approval on the ability of the indias to spin, dye, and weave woolen fabrics and sew. It was the women who did the farming and made the alcoholic beverages.[3] Slightly later Francisco Núñez de Pineda y Bascuñán told of females at work and play in their southern homes.[4]

The Jesuit historian, Alonso de Ovalle, pictured the traditional dress of the Araucanian india in 1646. The basic garment was a sleeveless, usually full-length, woolen tunic fastened at the shoulders with two silver pins or buckles and girdled with a wide sash. When she went outside her home, the woman covered her shoulders with a half-mantle or short cloak; a third silver clasp held it in place. Although indias wore neither shoes nor stockings, those who were becoming hispanized in the cities were adding footwear and some garments in the Spanish style to their wardrobes, but they were not adopting the gaudier fashions. The author frankly admired the simple, modest attire of the Indian women.[5]

His fellow Jesuits, Juan Ignacio Molina and Felipe Gómez de Vidaurre, borrowed freely from his description of Araucanian clothing, and, in the eighteenth-century spirit of the Enlightenment, strove for objectivity in evaluating Araucanian customs. Both were struck by the absolute dominance of the male and noted that husbands and fathers were not punished for killing wives or daughters. Quite obviously the Araucanian man commanded respect and subservience from his women. Since he devoted himself almost exclusively to military activities, much work that men did in other societies fell to the women, who not only took care of cooking, making clothes, and meticulous house cleaning but performed other essential tasks to support the family. According to Gómez de Vidaurre, it was very often left to the wives to do the plowing, and they always sowed and cultivated the fields and reaped the harvests. Women were in charge of the livestock and consequently sheared the sheep, milked the cows, and tended the horses. It was also their task to cut firewood and bring it to the home.[6] The Araucanian males, fabled for their stout resistance to conquest, surely fought for many reasons, but perhaps one motivation was to avoid being condemned to doing "women's work" for Spaniards.

The modern day anthropologist could add many refinements to these simplistic accounts of the division of labor between the sexes, but the indias in the several regions of Chile had developed occupational skills before the coming of the Caucasian and Negroid immigrants that were modified through contacts with the newcomers. Many females would be constrained to apply their skills for Hispanic masters or mistresses as their forebears had worked for their Indian husbands.

Some non-Chilean Indians came to the southern colony with the early expeditions. Both Almagro and Valdivia brought male and female Peruvian Indians with them. The women, some of whom were concubines, were for the most part those servants permanently bound to a household and were known as *yanaconas*. As the Spaniards founded municipalities, local women were also commandeered into this type of servitude. Some historians formerly viewed the yanaconas as surrogate members of Spanish families,[7] and, while it is true that an occasional will contained bequests to male and female yanaconas,[8] their status in terms of mobility and redress of grievances was scarcely removed from slavery. Their relationship with the head of the household was more akin to that of owner to slave than employer to employee.[9]

In addition to the yanaconas, some Chilean Indians were outright slaves. Seventeenth-century laws which legalized the enslavement of prisoners captured in the Araucanian war allowed males and females, young and old, to be condemned to bondage. The legislation authorizing Indian slavery and formally abolishing it is summarized in Chapter 3.

Another form of Indian servitude was encomienda service, and the role of Indian women in the history of the encomienda in Chile, like the institution itself, underwent many modifications.[10] An individual who received a writ of encomienda had certain responsibilities toward the Indians, and the adult males in turn owed tribute in labor, produce, or money. But the Indian men had wives and daughters, and the villages where they lived included widows and single women. The indias were legally exempt from rendering tribute, yet, in fact, women and girls often worked to meet the tribute levies.

Indian society had its own hierachy, and royal legislation conceded privileges to village headmen (caciques) and their wives and families. For example, these persons were free of tribute obligations. In recognition of their rank, Indian leaders were entitled to more land and better clothing than commoners. However, rank and privilege, in many instances, came to have a hollow ring as Indian society met with ever increasing pressure from the European presence. The number of commoners subject to a cacique decreased and, even if a village (*pueblo*) survived, the size of landholdings diminished.

In the Spanish cities there was a corresponding increase in the number of displaced persons who were neither slaves, yanaconas, nor members of encomiendas. Many females from this group found employment in Spanish households, practiced crafts, or worked in various types of retailing. By the late sixteenth century, those who did not find jobs were put to work through the contract system.

In both the urban and rural areas, Indian women voluntarily or under duress, took males from the various racial and ethnic groups as sexual partners. Whether through marriage, consensual union,

35

concubinage, or rape, the offspring of racially mixed parentage or ancestry constituted a growing segment of the population whose social status was defined in a hundred subtle ways, including income, lifestyle, and even clothing. At one end of the scale stood Ana María Loyola y Coya, the very young daughter of Governor Martín García Oñez de Loyola and his wife, Beatriz Clara Coya, an Inca princess. Although this mother and daughter had a brief sojourn in Chile, they had little in common with the local indias and mestizas. An enormous social gulf separated them from the hispanized mestiza, Agueda Flores, wife of the influential Pedro Lisperguer and daughter of Elvira, the *cacica* (Indian headwoman) of Talagante, and the German conquistador Bartolomé Flores. No Chilean mestizas could equal Ana María Loyola y Coya's rank, and few could rival Agueda's standing. Some might be found in middle income groups but most were poor and often regarded as an adjunct of Indian society. As previously indicated, zambas faced serious barriers to social and economic advancement.

The general condition of the Indian woman and her daughters was not unique to Chile and parallels could be cited in most, if not all, of the Spanish dominions. It is equally true that social gradations and regional differences between the Indians of the dry north, the villagers of the Central Valley, and the multiple peoples who lived in the mountains, forests, and coastal areas of the south belie attempts to generalize about the female experience. Accordingly the following chapters serve as an introduction to the subject with primary emphasis on the indias.

Chapter 3
Abuses and Protective Measures

The Indian woman, subjugated by her father and husband in her own world, came under a new and alien domination with the advance of the Spanish forces in Chile. At the same time, Spaniards trained in the principles of Christian humanism strove to mitigate the ravages of conquest and included women in their struggle to achieve a measure of justice for the Chilean Indian. Abuses of females that evoked repeated criticism, especially in the Hapsburg centuries, were sexual exploitation, excessive compulsory labor sometimes exacted through harsh punishments, and actual enslavement. Most of the advocates of reform were ecclesiastics, but a few were well intentioned public officials. The pro-indigenists had no common set of specific goals or unified reform program, but through their efforts various decrees, ordinances, and *tasas* (tribute assessments) were enacted with the hope of limiting if not eliminating exploitation of both men and women. However, uneven and ineffective enforcement weakened the impact of the legislation and prevented it from working any fundamental change in the condition of the Indian woman.[1] The following summary of the legal regimen bears this out. Besides indicating the types of abuses perpetrated and the steps taken to correct them, it also reveals the restrictive and repressive side of the law itself.

Writs of encomienda were important legal documents entrusting Indians to Spaniards and stipulating the relationship between them. The writs stated that Indian caciques could retain their wives, children, and servants; however, they did not protect female commoners in any particular way or guarantee that married couples and families would not be separated. The typical encomienda title contained only a vague, general mandate to the encomendero to observe the regulations on tribute, obey the royal commands and ordinances on the good treatment and conservation of the Indians, and see to their instruction in the Catholic faith.[2] Even these simple rules were all too frequently ignored.

Since Chile had no indigenous draft animals, Indians in a very real, physical sense had to bear the burdens of conquest. Both Almagro and Valdivia had used Peruvian Indian porters on their expeditions, but Valdivia, once he began to found settlements, banned the use of women for carrying cargo. The prohibition had no more effect than his early attempt to prevent women from being sent to the gold mines.[3]

The first major attack on these dehumanizing abuses came during the administration of Governor García Hurtado de Mendoza and was the work of the licentiate, Hernando de Santillán y Figueroa, an oidor of Lima on assignment as the chief justice of Chile. He drafted two sets of regulations, one for the encomiendas in La Serena and Santiago and the other for the southern regions. In line with previous royal legislation, he outlawed the use of female porters, and all women and children were henceforth to be exempt from mining labor. It was permissible, however, in the south to send a limited number of indias to the mines as cooks. Spaniards throughout Chile could have female servants in their homes if the women received compensation. Men assigned to work on a rotational basis in mining, farming, or ranching tasks were also to be reimbursed. Santillán wanted to limit the type and amount of work that Spaniards could exact and to leave the Indian villagers sufficient free time to support themselves, and he took care to add that the encomenderos had to furnish religious instruction to all the villagers and see to their medical needs.[4]

With no systematic enforcement mechanism and rapid turnovers in the governorship, it is not surprising that the Santillán legislation proved little more than a dead letter. In the 1570s Bishop Diego de Medellín of Santiago visited his diocese and found that females of all ages as well as men were not only being forced to work on their encomenderos' rural lands but were treated atrociously.[5]

In 1579 the caciques and commoners of the encomienda of Juan de Cuevas had an opportunity to report on him during an official inspection. The investigation produced a census which showed that many Indians lacked baptismal names and listed multiple cases of concubinage and polygamy — indicating that the encomendero was not overly zealous about his duty regarding the conversion of his wards to Christianity. When questioned about their treatment, the Indians answered that neither the encomendero nor his employees inflicted corporal punishment on them, nor were their wives and children being commandeered. However, some family groups had been sent to a mining camp. An Indian mother reported that her daughter Catalina was "in service," but she did not stipulate where the eighteen-year-old woman worked.[6] After the on-site interviews, an official accused the encomendero of extorting unwarranted labor and claimed that Juan de Cuevas did not pay the Indian women who made pottery jugs for him. Juan responded that only one Indian man had worked as a potter, and he had been paid. The encomendero thought it was justifiable for Indians to do agricultural work because it was the source of their own food supply. Moreover, poor Indian widows and orphans also received sustenance in that fashion.[7]

One purpose of the inspection had been to discover if there were a need for new regulations to replace the Santillán measures.[8] Provisional Governor Martín Ruiz de Gamboa, who believed the time had come for a revision, promulgated the Tasa de Gamboa in 1580, but his brief tenure and opposition from encomenderos spelled defeat for his reform efforts which outlawed "personal service."[9]

Governor Alonso de Sotomayor had a decade to undo Gamboa's program and allowed encomenderos to put male and female Indians to work. Although the Spaniards had to provide some remuneration and religious instruction, the effect of Sotomayor's ordinances was to endorse the personal service that Indians performed without any effective limitations on the encomenderos' authority.[10] According to the cathedral chapter of Santiago, the governor himself was guilty of separating married couples when he assigned them to work for Spaniards.[11]

If Sotomayor legalized the forced labor that the encomenderos had demanded from the beginning, his successor, Martín García Oñez de Loyola, placed restraints on the Spaniards. His predecessors had appointed officials to supervise encomienda activity and Indian property; Oñez de Loyola, who wanted to put some distance between the encomendero and the Indians, thought that the proper personnel, operating under strict guidelines, could keep the encomendero at arm's length from the villagers.[12]

Of the several steps he took to implement that goal the most notable, from the standpoint of the indias, was an ordinance concerning the administrators of Indian villages.[13] The lengthy document dealt with the needs of both soul and body. For example, it outlawed work on Sundays and ordered the administrator to bring males and females together for religious services. They would recite Christian doctrine lessons each Wednesday and Friday before work. Every month the administrator was to hold a fiesta and distribute meat allotments to the villagers, including widows. Since the latter had chácaras, the official had to see to it that the crops on their small farms were tended.

The governor hoped to preserve the Indian communities and therefore instructed the administrators to return absentee males and females to the villages. He evidently realized that some officials might arbitrarily separate married couples or prevent marriages, so he banned the use of force and intimidation against Indians whose spouses came from other pueblos because coercion would violate their liberty. The administrator should, nevertheless, advise Indians to marry persons from their own villages in order to conserve and augment them. As a final caution in this regard, Governor Oñez de Loyola declared that experience had shown that indias who married outside their home pueblos were mistreated.

The remainder of the regulations concerning women pertained to labor and again showed a respect for Indian marriage. No Indian wives could be sent to Santiago as nursemaids; the protector of the Indians, not the administrator, would take charge of hiring out single women for that purpose.

Wayside inns dotted the roadways of colonial Chile, and the Indian women customarily assigned to staff them came under the governor's scrutiny. Neither wives, untrustworthy women, nor young girls could work in them. Only single women over forty years of age were approved for inn labor and they were to return to their own houses to sleep at night.

The priest of the district could employ an unmarried fifty-year-old servant woman provided that he paid her two garments per year. The administrator himself could have one male and one female servant, but no other Indians whatsoever could work for him. He had to furnish the stipend that the servants owed for religious expenses and provide each of them with two garments, food, and medical care.

A separate ordinance directed to the protectors of the Indians spelled out their duties and instructed them to check up on the administrators by consulting with caciques and the wisest villagers. Together the protector, priest, and administrator of each pueblo would defend its men, women, and children from the men who came to the Central Valley for military supplies[14] and whose activities were a frequent source of complaint.

The ordinances on administrators and protectors conformed to the ideals which Oñez de Loyola set out in a proclamation concerning the good treatment of Indians. He exhorted officials and private individuals alike to respect the rights of the Indians, treat them well, and refrain from inflicting harm on their wives, children, and property. He wanted Indian families to enjoy liberty and security in their homes while they tended to their affairs and acquired the means to pay the tributes due the encomenderos.[15] The last statement was obviously intended to remind the Spaniards that good treatment was clearly in their own self interest.

No one was more aware than the governor that many Spaniards were giving free rein to the profit motive in enslaving Indians. Had he overlooked the nefarious practice, which began in the earliest days of the conquest and became more prevalent on the Araucanian frontier, Bishop Agustín de Cisneros of Imperial stood ready to inform the governor, as he had the king, of that illegal activity. In a letter to Philip II in 1590, Cisneros lamented the way married couples and families were separated when soldiers conducted slave raids (malocas) to procure male and female servants and obtain women for their "immoral purposes."[16] Oñez de Loyola worked to stop the exportation of southern Indians to the Central Valley, but his lack of success is apparent in one of his last letters to the crown which described how women and girls as well as men and boys were still being transported to Santiago under the most dehumanizing circumstances.[17]

One of the saddest of all colonial documents came out of the traffic in Indian slaves. The transaction it recorded took place on April 14, 1605, when two men met to close a business deal. Diego de Cartagena traded a horse and "the services" of a female child approximately four years old, who had been captured in the war, to Blas Pereira for the services of a boy named Blasillo. If, within a year, the girl died or someone else proved title to her, Diego would pay Blas thirty pesos. The Chilean scholar, Alvaro Jara discovered three other cases of female prisoners of war being sold in Satiago in 1607 and 1608; each was identified by name.[18] Only the little girl worth thirty pieces of silver remained an anonymous victim of war and greed.

The enslavement of Araucanian rebels and pacified southern villagers, even those allied with the Spaniards, was soon to reach outrageous proportions. A general Indian uprising which began in 1598 with the death of Governor Oñez de Loyola in battle drove the Spanish settlers from all the southern cities except Concepción and Castro by 1604. This rebellion gave the anti-indigenists the arguments they wanted for a harsh Indian policy, and in 1608 the crown legalized the enslavement of all prisoners of war including males over ten and one-half and females over nine and one-half years of age.[19]

The decree was subsequently rescinded for a time and new measures pronounced many of the captives free.[20] However, a second royal law in 1622 again authorized the enslavement of any Indians, male or female, who attacked Spaniards; only children under fourteen years of age were exempted.[21] The Pact of Quillín effected between Governor Francisco López de Zúñiga, the Marqués de Baides, and leading Araucanian caciques in 1641 promised an end to slave raids and forced labor,[22] but the crown did not formally abolish Indian slavery in Chile until Queen Regent Mariana decreed total abolition in 1674. Governor Juan Henríquez, rather than set the Indians free, merely placed them in the custody of their former owners. Charles II allowed the system of "depositing" Indians in this manner to continue, and the custodians were satisfied with the compromise.[23]

Although the crown had never condoned the wholesale enslavement of the southern tribes, rapacious soldiers and officials, including some governors, and, on occasion, Indian allies paid scant attention to the fine points of the law when they scoured the frontier on slave raids to apprehend men, women, and children.[24] Some slavers abandoned any pretext of capturing prisoners in a "just war" and simply purchased women and children from their parents in order to enslave them for their own service or to sell them to colonists eager to obtain servitors.[25]

Law and justice did occasionally triumph and restore liberty to persons wrongfully reduced to bondage. A royal cédula directed to the bishop of Santiago on December 5, 1675, to correct an abuse perpetrated before the abolition decree, described one of those rare instances. The crown was replying to a letter from the oidor Juan de la Peña Salazar concerning a free Indian woman named Margarita, unlawfully enslaved by one Cristóbal Ponce and caught in a whirl-pool of factional discord and jurisdictional disputes. Peña Salazar, commissioned as visitor general for an inspection of the realm, had accepted Margarita's case against Cristóbal and issued a preliminary ruling upholding the liberty of the woman and her son. The audiencia, however, summoned her to Santiago for a hearing. When she returned, the visitor general again ruled in her favor, but before he could issue a final verdict, Juan Henríquez, the governor and president of the audiencia, recalled Margarita to Santiago. In spite of Peña Salazar's remonstrances against her taking an arduous journey while she was ill, the president and oidores prevailed. It was this final perversion of justice that prompted action in Madrid when Peña Salazar's letter arrived. The queen mother, aware of the feud between the governor and the visitor general, needed a neutral party to investigate and consequently authorized the bishop to discover whether Henríquez and the high court had indeed ordered Margarita back to Santiago. If so, he was to levy a fine of 500 pesos against their salaries with the governor paying double the sum assessed each judge. Margarita was to receive the money as "satisfaction for the grievance and molestations" done her.[26] The interposition of royal authority was unfortuntely too infrequent to have any widespread effect, however. Even in this case, the documents fail to mention whether Margarita was actually paid.

Since so much slaving activity was illegal, few statistical records were kept, and, as a result, the number of female Indian slaves is not known. However, a report on the slave traffic in 1656 indicated that adult women were considered twice as valuable as men. At that time, women and young males commanded a price of 200 pesos in contrast to adult males and children under the age of 10 who were selling for only 100 pesos.[27]

While the slavers declared open season on their prey, the pro-indigenists and anti-indigenists who lobbied against each other on the slavery issue also debated the question of obligatory personal service which was so analogous to slavery as to be virtually indistinguishable from it. Proponents of social justice, many of them Jesuit priests, won some reforms for the servitors who were technically free as distinct from the slaves, but compulsory labor persisted.[28]

The most significant attempt to ease the burden of personal service in Chile was the Tasa of Esquilache, enacted in 1620, under the auspices of the Viceroy of Peru, Francisco de Borja y Aragón, the Prince of Esquilache. Although Indian males were still liable for some compulsory labor, women and children were exempt from any obligatory service. However, they could voluntarily work for wages, and women employed as domestic servants were henceforth to receive not only food, living quarters, and medical care but wages payable in clothes or textiles. Servants were to be free to marry, and a woman under a year's contract to an employer could go to live with her husband when the contract expired. Those women working in the forts on the southern frontier were to have a separate barracks to protect them from sexual exploitation.[29] Although the tasa was never fully implemented,[30] Philip IV confirmed most of the ordinances in 1622, and his version became the royal tasa which made its way into the *Recopilación* published later in the century.[31]

That compilation of law took no notice of the new ordinances enacted in 1635 by Governor Francisco Lazo de la Vega to supplement the royal tasa. His regulations ostensibly complied with a royal directive to abolish personal service but actually penalized any males who attempted to pay tribute to their encomenderos in cash. As recent scholarship has shown, the measures thus failed to alleviate Indian labor. Lazo de la Vega, according to the Chilean historian, Mario Góngora, also made it easier for encomenderos to move Indian villagers to the estancias and chacras that Spaniards owned.[32] The governor did, however, enjoin encomenderos and others who had Indians working for them to treat both men and women "as vassals of His Majesty and free persons," and facilitate their Chritianization and practice of the faith. Alcoholic abuse particularly concerned the governor, and he threatened severe penalties to any Spaniards who allowed Indians to obtain wine. Neither could whites do business with Indian males to acquire their clothes or those of their wives and children. Indian men, on the other hand, were admonished to live like "Catholic Christians and vassals of His Majesty." They were to work to support themselves, earn "clothing for their wives and children," and avoid drunkenness "and vices and sins."[33]

When the *Recopilación* came off the press in 1681, it included those portions of the earlier royal tasa that pertained to the Christianization of Chilean Indians as well as the clauses which spoke of their rights and duties. For example, the legislation described how rural churches would be built and staffed with priests whose salaries would come from a portion of the Indian tribute. While priests bore the primary responsibility for holding religious services and giving instructions, in the latter instance they were to have the aid of a bright Indian youth. In the cities, Indian servants had to have opportunities to attend Mass on Sundays and Holy Days as well as religion classes.[34]

The spirit, and, in some cases, the letter of the royal legislation was upheld when Bishop Bernardo Carrasco y Saavedra of Santiago convoked the diocesan synod of 1688 to deal with spiritual, moral, and ethical questions. This is apparent in the pronouncements directed to the clergy and laity of the diocese.[35]

All pastors were to teach Christian doctrine to Indian men and women each Sunday and Holy Day not only to explain the mysteries of the faith but to preach against vices, especially drunkenness and sensuality.[36] Civil officials were to seek ways to deal with Indian alcoholism.[37] The synod itself set the closing hours for stores and taverns in order to prevent the public sins occasioned by the dissolute women of the several ethnic groups, pejoratively called *lusitanas*.[38]

Spaniards were to send their workers and servants to the special religious instructions given in the cities on the Sundays in Lent and Advent. In the rural areas, regular religion classes for Indians were to meet twice each week. A capable Indian boy would teach prayers and the catechism to young girls and women; single men and adult women would learn Christian doctrine. Priests, encomenderos, administrators of Indian villages, and estate managers were to make sure that the young tutors were available to perform their duties as directed in the royal tasa.[39]

Before any nonwhite adults could receive the sacraments of baptism, penance, Holy Eucharist, and confirmation, they had to memorize the Lord's Prayer and the Creed and know the cathechism available in the diocese in the Spanish and Indian languages. Priests were to work actively to see that both Afro-Chileans and Indians mastered these basic requirements.[40]

On the estancias, a well-instructed layman was to lead the Indians and blacks in reciting prayers and the catechism each morning before work. Landowners and estate managers were to see to attendance; any of these Spaniards who obstructed the recitations would be fined, and if he still proved recalcitrant, punished with excommunication. Each month, rural priests were to visit their charges, instructing the faithful in person and taking special notice of the sick.[41]

The synod participants were deeply concerned that Indians not face death without the consolation of the last rites. Accordingly they admonished priests to administer the sacraments to Indian men and women who were gravely ill.[42]

The Santiago city council, when asked to suggest topics for the synod's agenda, had remonstrated against reprehensible priests who inveigled bequests from Indians on their deathbeds.[43] Since Church leaders also wanted to protect Indians from falling victim to clerical extortion, the synod reaffirmed existing prohibitions of simony and financial regulations which exempted Indian villagers as individuals from specific fees for funerals, baptisms, and marriages. Neither could a parish priest inherit property from an Indian man or woman.[44]

The city councilmen had also criticized the high incidence of concubinage, especially among Indians, and the way persons living in such illicit unions flaunted the sanctity of marriage.[45] The synod treated those subjects in several enactments that upheld traditional Church teachings. In the first place, priests were reminded, under threat of heavy penalties, to be most circumspect in their dealings with all women in order to avoid even the hint of clerical concubinage. Moreover, they could not employ young women or girls as servants.[46]

In an obvious effort to prevent the laity from entering bigamous unions, the synod ruled that only the bishop could grant a dispensation from the publication of the banns of matrimony.[47] Couples from all the ethnic groups were to have the nuptial blessing no later than six days after the exchange of wedding vows. Marriages, funerals, confirmations, and baptisms were to be carefully recorded.[48] As mentioned earlier, the synod also expounded on the right of Afro-Chileans to marry. Any Spaniard who impeded the freedom of Indians or black slaves to marry or forced them into a marriage against their will would be excommunicated with absolution reserved to the bishop.[49]

Labor questions figured prominently in the synodal legislation. For example, men and women who had household servants were exhorted to relieve them of working at night. Neither the laity nor the clergy could force Indians or blacks to work on feast days without compensation; if they freely desired to do so, wages had to be paid under penalty of excommunication. In cases of dire necessity, compulsory labor for wages could be required after obtaining ecclesiastical permission.[50] These latter prohibitions were less enlightened than they appear because, at the city council's insistence, some of the many feast days that required abstinence from manual labor did not apply in the rural areas.[51]

The synod twice mentioned the restrictions on labor set in the royal tasa earlier in the century. In the first place, rural priests were to see to it that Indians received good treatment and were not worked above and beyond the limitations established in the royal legislation. Secondly, encomenderos and estate managers were to observe those limits.[52]

Although king and Church tried to reduce the amount of labor an encomendero could demand, the crown was still trying to reach that objective in the early 1700s.[53] The synod may have touched the consciences of some individual Spaniards, but it did not reverse the prevailing pattern of exploitation as the king and the Council of the Indies learned when they studied the Chilean situation in 1703. Correspondence from civil officials and the Bishop of Santiago, Francisco de la Puebla González, described the "miserable condition" and declining numbers of the Indians. A major reason for this state of affairs was the fact that encomenderos inflicted bad treatment through "personal service, working them by day and by night without rest, and without giving them a place in which to reside with their wives and children," and taking away their daughters as servants.[54] The bishop thought and the king so ruled, in spite of contrary advice from some Chilean officials, that the creation of Indian pueblos under the jurisdiction of a corregidor would resolve these problems. However, new villages that were established were enclaves within estancias owned by whites.[55] The only solution to the abuse of personal service was the final abolition of the encomienda itself in 1791.[56]

The legislative attempts to interpose civil authority between the Indian and the encomendero spoke to the need to substitute a rule of law for the personalist control the Spaniard exerted. The fiscal of the audiencia, Pedro Machado de Cháves, called attention to this in 1634. After he reported in a letter to the king that the wives of encomenderos tyrannized over their Indian female servants and beat them, he asked the judges of the high court to levy a fine of 500 pesos on any person who flogged either Indian men or women. Although his proposal was voted down,[57] the Tasa of Lazo de la Vega stipulated that magistrates, not private individuals, would punish Indians who committed crimes.[58]

This did not prevent cruelty, but endeavors to give Indians access to the courts had some positive results. For example, Isabel Ponce León de Varas in 1647 gave orders for an Indian woman who worked for her to be beaten because she married in defiance of the wishes of her encomendera, Lorenza Vásquez. The audiencia accepted the suit that the protector of the Indians brought on behalf of the servant.[59] The case is doubly significant because it involved not only the india's right to marry but the principle of accountability for harsh treatment.

The charges against Isabel came at a time when the audiencia and Governor Martín Mujica were taking an interest in correcting abuses against servant women.[60] The verdict in her case is not known, but the arm of the law was never long or strong enough to eliminate arbitrary punishment. In 1713 a cacique from the encomienda of Blas de los Reyes complained that the latter employed corporal punishment. The encomendero defended himself with the rationalization that he used the same type of correction that parents used with their children. The encomendero's attitude and behavior assumed the right to enforce his will on subordinates without recourse to any formal legal proceedings.[61]

Corporal punishment was, of course, nothing unusual as far as nonwhites were concerned. Municipal ordinances, as already explained, showed a shocking, if routine, severity in defining and punishing crimes committed by Indians, blacks, and castes. When threatening nonwhites with harsh penalties, the councilmen presumably intended for those accused of an offense to be tried in a magistrate's court.

A problem in the judicial and administrative system was to find personnel who would deal fairly with the Indians. Many of the local officials in charge of Indian affairs obtained their posts through gubernatorial patronage. That influential Spaniards could coopt the system is clearly demonstrated in the appointment of Doña Antonia de Aguilera y Estrada, the wife of Fernando de Irarrázaval y Zárate, as the administrator of the Indians and pueblo of Rapel. Governor Lazo de la Vega empowered her to exercise the office or to name a person to act in her stead. Antonia chose the latter course, and her appointee, Alonso Truchado, posted bond and presented his credentials to the cabildo. These included not only the original appointment and her notarized delegation of authority to him but a receipt for the payment of the *mesada* (a tax on offices). Since the papers were in order, the city council authorized him to take up his duties on February 23, 1630.[62] For a woman to obtain any political office was extremely rare. Antonia's designation as the titular administrator had further significance in the fact that the Indians placed under her jurisdiction belonged to the encomienda that she and her husband held.

The villagers of Pacoa as well as those of Rapel had been consigned to men in the Irarrázaval-Zárate family in the sixteenth century. The Indians were on the point of escheating to the crown when the widow, Lorenza de Zárate y Recalde, by virtue of a monetary payment to the royal treasury obtained a new writ of encomienda from the viceroy of Peru for her very young son, Fernando, in 1593. At one point, Lorenza became the administrator of the Indians, but it is not clear whether this referred to her capacity as a surrogate encomendera or to special duties as a civil official. In any event, Fernando gave up the encomienda when he was absent from Chile for an extended period. A new viceregal title to the Indians of Rapel and Pacoa went to Catalina Niño de Estrada whose daughter, Antonia de Aguilera y Estrada, was their encomendera when Fernando returned to Chile. For her marriage to Fernando in 1620, Antonia's dowry included a large rural estate in the district of Rapel. He no doubt assumed the role of encomendero until he died in 1632, while serving as the corregidor of Arequipa in Peru. Antonia, who had stayed at home with their children, again became the encomendera.[63] Her personal interest in the encomienda and the opportunity to place a lackey in the office of administrator of Rapel gave Antonia de Aguilera a formidable authority over the Indians and their properties. This is not to say, however, that her appointee was necessarily any worse than other members of the civil hierarchy.

The temptation to use authority for private gain or illicit purposes extended from the administrators of pueblos, city councilmen, corregidores, and protectors of Indians to the governor and audiencia ministers. When allowances are made for the tendency of disgruntled colonists and political rivals to exaggerate charges of official misconduct, the historical record still returns a strong indictment against the quality of the bureaucracy.

In 1630 the bishop of Santiago reported that the fiscal and judges of the audiencia assigned Indian male and female servants to themselves and their friends and relatives.[64] The high court in 1623 had heard a similar case against a corregidor in the province of Cuyo.[65] Testimony from three indias was admitted as evidence in 1678 against the corregidor of that trans-Andean province who stood accused of multiple charges, including chasing after Indian women and attempted rape.[66] The fact that female Indians could bear witness against an official is noteworthy but does not obscure the reality of female vulnerability to unscrupulous bureaucrats.

In 1616 the administrator of Indian villages in the district of Maule, south of Santiago, reported to his superior, the protector of the Indians, that the corregidor had allowed the encomendero, Juan de las Cuevas, to take Indians from a village for service as yanaconas. Since some of the men fled, Juan took the wife and children of one of the fugitives, even though it was the middle of winter and the mother had recently delivered a child. The administrator, who himself faced various accusations,[67] had thought to appear in a better light by exposing the misdeeds of the corregidor and the encomendero.

A corregidor of Cuyo, who was under investigation for accepting bribes, followed a similar tactic. He informed the fiscal of the audiencia that a certain Juan Jufré de Estrada had been living in concubinage with an Indian woman for four years. When Juan's wife, a lady of exemplary life, asked the corregidor to correct the situation, he had the concubine arrested and confined in jail in irons. Since Juan was determined to free his beloved india, the corregidor maintained an around-the-clock guard of four men. The aggrieved wife, fearing that her husband would try to murder her, again asked for help. However, when the corregidor tried to arrest Juan at his home, the culprit escaped through an orchard. The fiscal's response in 1653 was an order for the guilty parties to be punished.[68] He neither explained how to untangle the questions of guilt or innocence nor suggested a suitable punishment. The Indian woman had already been subjected to a rigorous jail sentence, and, as Asunción Lavrin has indicated, it was not unusual for women accused of sexual immorality in Spanish America to draw heavier penalties than men.[69]

Civil judges and administrators as well as ecclesiastics routinely dealt with questions of morality and religion. It was not only the royal patronage of the Church and the deliberate creation of overlapping jurisdictions but also the Spanish value system that accounted for this. The intricate relationship between Church and State on every level and the importance of Catholicism in daily life inevitably had an effect on indias and mestizas. For example, the priestly chroniclers of Chilean history rejoiced at the devout lives of Indians admitted to the Christian fold and described the activities of their religious confraternities.[70] In contrast, the Holy Office recorded sordid tales of priests who elicited sexual favors from indias and mestizas and of laymen who considered fornication with Indian women either no sin at all or at most a venial sin. Punishment and penance were, of course, meted out to those the Inquisition found guilty of sin and error.[71]

The burden of discrimination that Chilean Indian women bore was almost insupportable. Failure to enforce protective legislation and diligence in taking advantage of the laws that were slanted against her, left the india on precarious ground — vulnerable to slave owner, encomendero, employer, officeholder, and even an occasional priest. The system, reflecting the prejudice of the age, unquestionably defeated many mestizas as well as indias who were unable to combat its rigors. Others, in spite of the handicaps that law and custom imposed, made significant contributions, especially in the economic sphere.

Chapter 4
Real Estate

The full story of the Indian and the colonial land question is only now unfolding as court cases and notarial records are searched more thoroughly to supplement previous findings.[1] Where the Indian woman fits into that narrative is the subject of the following discussion which cites instances of private ownership of both rural and urban real estate and takes note of the communal lands that rural pueblos held and the plots assigned to individual villagers.

One of the better known Indians in the conquest era was the Peruvian woman, Inés González. She figured prominently in the same smear campaign against the cleric Rodrigo González Marmolejo in 1556 that implicated him in the marital cases concerning the mulata, Catalina de Mella. It was alleged that he had lived with Inés as his concubine, gave her gold that his Indian work gangs mined, and continued the affair after he married her off to an Indian named Alonso, who already had a wife. The charges and inconclusive testimony proved only that the priest had an Indian servant named Inés but nothing about the illicit relationship or his lavishing ill-gotten wealth on her.[2] Inés adopted his surname, however, and the clergyman, who is spite of his detractors became the first bishop of Santiago, gave her a chacra on the outskirts of the city. When she wrote her will and codicils in 1564, Inés mentioned the farm and declared that she owned houses on two city lots as well as eleven mares and colts, ten goats, ten sheep, and a small herd of swine. She bequeathed part of the real estate to thirteen of her Indian relatives and associates who had worked the farm with the assistance of her ten yanaconas.[3] The fact that Inés González, a woman of some means, not only used a Spanish name and acquired Indian servitors, real property, and livestock but also prepared testamentary dispositions indicates that she had accommodated herself to the Hispanic way of life. In this she was similar to sixteenth-century Indian women of

Arequipa, Peru, whose ability to take advantage of conditions during the conquest has been studied by Elinor C. Burkett.[4]

A few Indians owned lots in Santiago's white neighborhoods in the sixteenth century. Among them in 1557 was a woman named María, who belonged to the encomienda of Diego García de Cáceres. A new neighborhood that was at first exclusively Indian was taking shape by 1560, and the city council issued titles to many city lots to both men and women; some married couples had joint ownership, and, in a number of cases, Indian children inherited the property from their parents.[5] As time passed, there was less city-owned land available for grants or sales, but as late as 1681 the council entertained a purchase offer tendered by the Indian woman, Luisa, a servant of the notary, Matías de Ugas. Luisa wanted to buy part of a lot that the municipality owned and was willing to pay the assessed price. Unfortunately, the council minutes do not tell whether she actually made the purchase.[6]

The Spanish practice of proving title to property with written deeds had its counterpart in Indian oral tradition that kept alive claims to property that, if less weighty than a formal title, were admissible in establishing rights to ownership or usage. A poignant example of this is contained in the records of the early seventeenth-century general land survey in the Central Valley. In 1604 the surveyor, Ginés de Lillo, used an interpreter to interview the oldest Indians from two pueblos to discover the traditional proprietorship of a disputed piece of land. One of the Indians, Bartolomé Panigueni, approximately seventy years old, recalled that his parents had told him of his birth in the land of Liray when it belonged to the Indians of the pueblo of Colina. His mother had gone there in search of food when she was pregnant, and he was born there.[7] The testimony thus demonstrated that Colina villagers were farming in the district in pre-conquest times, since the young Indian mother's quest for food roughly coincided with Almagro's entry into Chile.

At the time of the survey, some of the most extensive landholdings belonged to Agueda Flores, one of the wealthier mestizas of the entire colonial period. A glance at her life sheds light on the alienation of Indian lands and offers clues to the process of cultural assimilation within the upper class. Agueda's conquistador-father, Bartolomé Flores, had hispanized his German surname, Blumenthal, as a sign of his acceptance of Spanish ways. Similarly, her grandfather who was the cacique of the Indian village of Talagante at the time of the conquest had taken the Christian name Bartolomé when he was baptized. It was this chieftain's daughter, Elvira, the cacica of

Talagante, who became Agueda's mother. Although the sequence of events is not entirely clear, there is ample documentation regarding the liaison between the Indian headwoman and Bartolomé Flores, the birth of their natural daughter, Agueda, and the German conquistador's obtaining encomiendas from Pedro de Valdivia that included the Talagante villagers, taking up residence in their pueblo, practicing his trade as a carpenter, and establishing an early mill. Bartolomé Flores also acquired real estate in Santiago and its rural environs.[8]

The details of Agueda's childhood in terms of where she was reared and how and what she was taught unfortunately remain one of the hidden pages of history. But her actions as an adult reveal that she was well-versed in Spanish legal procedures and customs. It was probably in the 1560s that she married the prominent German immigrant, Pedro Lisperguer, in a formal ceremony blessed by the Church. She and Pedro had five sons and three daughters, including Catalina, the mother of the infamous "La Quintrala" de los Ríos.[9]

In 1585 Agueda's father named her his sole heiress in his will, obliging her to respect his bequests to his encomienda Indians. When he died, Agueda accordingly inherited his real property. The Flores Indians were added to previous encomienda grants that Pedro Lisperguer had received in his own name.[10]

Ten years later Pedro Lisperguer, who was often absent in Peru, was again in Lima. Agueda wanted to join him and thought it prudent to draw up a will in 1595 because of the hazards of the planned journey. The will, notarized by Ginés de Toro Mazote, was quite similar to those drafted by Spaniards. In addition to alms and pious bequests for charitable and religious purposes, it allocated specific pieces of real property to Agueda's children who would share the residue of the posthumous estate equally. A slave woman named María and her two daughters were to serve Agueda's daughters because, as the testator declared, the slaves, who were presumably Afro-Chileans because the will antedated the legalization of Indian slavery, had been born and reared in her house. She bequeathed livestock to most of the encomienda Indians, but those of Talagante would receive 100 pesos in cloth while the same sum was set aside for the Indians working on her farm and serving as shepherds. This bequest was a tacit admission that Agueda, who would live to write another will or codicil in 1632,[11] and her husband had taken Indians from their homes.

Whether Agueda actually went to Peru is unknown, but her husband was there in the early seventeenth century. Since she was no doubt accustomed to handling the family enterprises while he was away, Agueda dealt with the land surveyor when Ginés de Lillo made his rounds through the Central Valley. She presented the appropriate papers to prove title to six pieces of rural land designated either as farms or ranches. Agueda had inherited some of the holdings from her father; others she owned jointly with her husband as community property. The documents showed, for example, that for over fifty years she, her father, and her husband had accumulated parcels of land some seven leagues from Santiago. Like many Spaniards, Agueda had the foresight to have their claims confirmed in a gubernatorial grant in 1595.[12] Another large piece of property, located on the road that carts plied from Santiago to the sea, required some research on the part of the surveyor because he studied the written records and interviewed elderly Indians before he authorized the placing of landmarks as boundaries. The land quite clearly belonged to Doña Agueda, he noted, but she must nonetheless allow the Talagante Indians to live on 200 *cuadras* (literally, blocks) for the remainder of her life. Although her husband had title to the encomienda, the surveyor called Agueda the Indians' *poseedora* (mistress, owner).[13] He did not explain whether he was acknowledging her rights as the heiress of the encomendero, Bartolomé Flores, and the cacica, Elvira of Talagante. Perhaps he meant to infer that Agueda had a special status not only because of her parents but also as a surrogate encomendera during her husband's absence.

The process of expropriation was well advanced by 1600, and the Talagante pueblo was apparently fully absorbed into the Lisperguer-Flores holdings when Agueda Flores' posthumous estate was divided among her heirs in 1633. The village had a small income of its own in 1618 but had lost any meaningful identity by 1639.[14]

The documentation compiled during the land survey in the early 1600s shows that something similar was happening throughout the Central Valley. As the surveyor proceeded with his work, Ginés de Lillo confirmed traditional, if diminished, holdings for a few villages other than Talagante.

The largest tract, comprising a grand total of 577 cuadras, went to the pueblo of Lampa. The village had 2 caciques who were each entitled to double plots. Male tributaries, married and single, numbered 66. There were 9 elderly men beyond the tributary age and 9 widows and single women. Since each cacique was to have 8 cuadras, and each of the enumerated commoners, 4, the individual plots accounted for 352 cuadras, while 225 cuadras were designated for communal usage.[15]

In a smaller village, the surveyor found 1 cacique, 24 tributaries, and 3 widows. He intended to give the cacique 8 cuadras, each tributary 4, and each widow 2 cuadras. With additional communal acreage, the village, called Pelvin "the new," obtained title to 200 cuadras.[16] The pueblo of Tango had even less land amounting to 160 cuadras.[17]

Indians in the village of Apoquindo that had belonged to the encomienda of the conquistadora, Inés Suárez, managed to retain some property into the early eighteenth century, but the village had disappeared by 1759. There were only a few Indians — 37 males and 3 widows — entitled to plots when Ginés de Lillo arrived there in 1603 and surveyed their holdings.[18]

The recognition of a widow's right to a parcel of land to help support her in her old age continued through the colonial period. A document dating from 1690 stated that the farming land for Indian villages included 10 cuadras for a cacique, 5 for each tributary, and 3 for each widow; however, the report sounded the ominous note that communal grazing lands had been granted to Spaniards.[19] In 1748 and 1759 officials in Santiago referred to the same allotments and indicated that the villages still owned some communal pastures[20]

The city council session of August 8, 1745, in the northern town of Copiapó included information from the corregidor on his recent population census and land survey of the pueblo of San Fernando. The village had a cacique, 42 men, and 6 widows who were assigned plots within the total of 334 cuadras. This was 83 cuadras less than the village had prior to the survey. The corregidor declared that the additional acreage was "vacant" and should be distributed to Spaniards or used as municipal property. The council approved, despite the cacique's objections to the loss of the land.[21]

For most of the pueblos, then, the retention of land was a losing struggle with fewer and fewer villagers owning less and less land as Spaniards augmented the size of their estates. As the following cases show, some indias and mestizas struggled against the alienation of private and communal holdings and others collaborated in the process.

The Indians who fought a war of attrition over land tenure included women like the cacica in the district of Aconcagua, Doña María Trejo. In the early seventeenth century, she received help from Governor Alonso García Ramón in a lawsuit with a Spaniard who asserted that he had been given a land grant that encompassed three pieces of her property.[22]

At approximately the same time, the acting cacique of the pueblo of

Malloa and his wife had title to land that their daughters, Gracia and Catalina, later inherited. Although the two women sold it to a Spaniard, the sale was annulled, and Gracia then sold her part to a Spanish woman.[23]

The mestizo Gonzalo Martínez de Vergara, son of Francisco Martínez and the cacica Mariana Pichunlien whose surname is also rendered Pico de Plata, inherited lands in Chacabuco that had belonged to his Indian forebears. One of his daughters eventually donated the rural holdings to the Jesuits.[24]

In the sixteenth century, Indians who lived near the residence that the conquistador Francisco de Aguirre owned in the small settlement of Copiapó wanted to sell property in order to obtain livestock. Two Indian women were involved in the preliminary steps: María Che, the wife of the cacique Francisco Guanitai, and Catalina, the mother of another Indian headman. Female Indian commoners attended a meeting on December 9, 1561, to discuss the matter of the sale. When an auction was held early in 1562, the high bid was thirty sheep, worth ten gold pesos each, for a house, an orchard, a vegetable garden, plus another piece of land. The Spanish purchaser then transferred the property to María de Torres, the wife of Francisco de Aguirre. However, the Indians still retained some lands in the area. The cacique, Francisco Guanitai, soon deeded over a lot for a parish church but kept the fields his subjects cultivated for him. His heiress, Ana Quismaichai, sold that farm to a Spaniard in 1580. Years later a descendant of the cacique, Bartolina Chillimaco, held title to some land when a Spaniard lodged a rival claim during a survey in 1712. The fiscal of the audiencia ruled Bartolina Chillimaco the true owner as the rightful heiress to the property.[25]

An Indian husband and wife donated a lot to the Franciscans in Copiapó in September, 1664. To do this they had the approval of the corregidor and the protector of the Indians.[26]

Through land grants, purchases, lawsuits, and gifts, individual Spaniards and religious orders obtained lands that had once belonged to Indians. Another major factor working to diminish Indian holdings was the encomenderos' desire to have Indian workers who were liable for personal service settled on their property. There was no uniform policy, but it became common for villagers to be taken from their homes and assigned parcels within the confines of the Spaniards' estancias.[27]

Indians did not always accept removal passively, and some of the leaders who resisted were women. For example, the widow of a cacique tried but failed to gain permission for a group of Indians to be returned to their former homes in the 1690s.[28]

In spite of pleas from pro-indigenists that stressed that the Indians should have their own separate villages where they could live their own lives with greater dignity and less exposure to corrupting influences, the uprooting of Indian families continued even in the face of specific and general royal legislation to the contrary.[29]

Chapter 5
The World of Work

The encomienda of Luis Jufré provides a convenient bridge between the topics of Indian real estate and occupations. The encomienda that Luis inherited from his conquistador-father, Juan Jufré, who boasted of its size and value in 1572,[1] is at present the one best documented on the complementary themes of land and labor.

Young Luis had not yet reached the age of majority when his father died and the direction of the encomienda fell to the boy's mother, Constanza de Meneses, his legal guardian. Constanza was still functioning in that capacity in 1582 when acting Governor Martín Ruiz de Gamboa addressed a special tasa to Luis Jufré as the titular encomendero and limited the amount of tribute from the Indian villages that comprised the encomienda. The governor specified not only the amounts of gold and commodities but also the number of household servants, each due a salary. Since a total of thirty-four male and female Indians were assigned to the "common service" of the encomendero's home,[2] various kinds of duties from household chores to ranch and farm work were probably envisioned.

In 1590 Luis found a way to enlarge his household staff, expand his authority over other Indian workers, and increase the number of his livestock. He convinced Governor Sotomayor that he needed Indians from his encomienda as yanaconas, and the obliging administrator changed the status of some of the Jufré Indians. Henceforth the new yanaconas, whose homes were in the village of Macul, would work on Luis Jufré's land and in his home and enterprises under his direction. Luis would take charge of the livestock that belonged to the cacique and commoners and, in return for his efforts, obtain a percentage of the natural increase of the flocks and herds. The protector of the Indians would have no jurisdiction over the yanaconas. As their compensation, Luis had to provide each man and his wife and children with two pieces of clothing annually and allow them to cultivate plots of land for their food. He was responsible for tending them when they became ill and seeing to their instructions in Catholicism.[3]

THE WORLD OF WORK

A decade later, Luis Jufré was seeking to increase the size of his estate. The village of Macul, located in the district of Ñuñoa where he and other members of his family owned extensive property, had so few residents that it seemed ripe for the picking, and Luis in 1600 obtained a land grant that encompassed the territory.[4] He had reckoned, however, without Barbola de Oropesa, the widow of the deceased cacique Martín. Before the land surveyor, Ginés de Lillo, reached Macul in October, 1603, Barbola had sued on behalf of her daughter Constanza, Martín's heiress, to regain the village holdings. Until the courts would issue a verdict, the surveyor ordered Luis to allow the two women and three or four other Indians native to the village to occupy and cultivate a plot of land within the Jufré estancia.[5] Indian occupancy and usage if not proprietorship received a tenuous, temporary guarantee because of Barbola de Oropesa's initiative. Luis Jufré, for the moment, had been checked in his drive to expropriate Indian land.

A move to restrict his exploitation of Indian labor was already underway before the land survey took place. In 1602 and 1603 an inspection of the Jufré estancia, textile sweatshop, and encomienda villages, including Macul, showed a total Indian population of 784 persons with 159 tributaries and 34 individuals, male and female, assigned to personal service. There were only 12 residents in Macul; a married woman with 3 daughters and an elderly male were apparently exempt from work, but 5 men of tributary age and 2 unmarried women, because they were now classified as yanaconas, were all subject to personal service. During the visitation, 10 indias were working on the Jufré estancia without any specific job descriptions. Since Governor Sotomayor's general ordinances which allowed some encomienda women to be thus employed were still in effect, the inspector had to determine if the encomendero exceeded the numerical limitations and whether he fulfilled his obligations to the Indians. It was discovered, for example, that Luis was not supplying adequate rations for the people in the textile sweatshop who complained that they lacked tools to cultivate their small plots, and, consequently, their wives were hard put to feed their families. The inspector proposed strict guidelines on the number of textile workers and personal servants. Of the latter, only 14 could be female: 10 adult women and 4 young girls. The encomendero's control over the Macul villagers would be lessened since only 2 Indians, a man and a woman, would be personal servants.[6]

Whether Luis Jufré obeyed the new rules is not known; however, he typified the Spanish ambition to profit from Indian labor. The range of feminine occupational skills meant that Indian women throughout Spanish Chile would be relegated to a variety of tasks. They worked in the fields just as peasant women did in Europe. Some were sent to the mines, in spite of early and later prohibitions against the use of women in that arduous labor. Others made pottery or processed commodities such as flax. Indian women could be found spinning fibers, weaving fabrics, and sewing clothes for their families or the encomendero whether at home or in the hateful textile sweatshops. When the wife of an encomienda tributary had to help support the family by raising chickens and utilizing her talent at spindle and loom, it was cited as an abuse in 1610.[7] The woman's reaction to hard times was, nevertheless, indicative of feminine resourcefulness.

Throughout the colonial period both mestizas and indias worked as household servants. Contractual employees, yanaconas, Indian slaves, and females from the encomiendas were recruited, often forcibly, as domestics. Although general housework and cooking were apparently the most common tasks, some individuals acted as nursemaids to young children.[8] In a letter to the king in 1707, Governor Francisco Ibáñez y Peralta stated that it was logical for encomenderos to conscript the daughters of their Indians for their households because the realm had no other servants. In the rest of the world it was possible to hire servants, but the Chilean Indians did not want to enter domestic service voluntarily; therefore, the encomenderos' practice was expedient and justifiable.[9] In his eagerness to exculpate the Spaniards who removed females from the encomienda villages, the governor overlooked the presence of women from the other ethnic groups who worked alongside the Indians. He also ignored the pro-indigenists who argued that taking young women from the villages was disruptive of Indian family life.[10]

Indian legisltation dating from 1647 took note of the fact that female Indian villagers tended sick members of their communities. The ordinances issued by Governor Martín de Mujica stated that the sick, if not admitted to the hospital, were to have medicines made available from communal funds and that Indian women would be in charge of dispensing the medication and providing nursing care.[11] The same governor showed an interest in improving the quality of life of Indian servant women in Hispanic homes, but the earthquake that struck Santiago in 1647 aborted those intentions.[12]

Encomenderos with Indians to spare from their households and enterprises not infrequently hired them out to other employers and pocketed the profits. Marina Ortiz de Gaete, Pedro de Valdivia's widow, practiced this form of abuse prohibited by royal law since 1529.[13]

However, both royal legislation and local custom countenanced the other type of contract labor, already discussed regarding Afro-Chileans, designed to prevent what Spaniards called vagabondage. Public officials were authorized to put unemployed persons, regardless of race or sex, to work. The typical contract stated its duration, usually one or two years, and stipulated compensation that for Indians generally consisted of two garments, food, medical care, and the employer's payment of the stipend due the Indian curacy. Some few contracts pledged a final bonus that might be more clothing, a set of buttons, or a small sum of money. Women alone, or with their husbands and children, entered such contracts which provided them with basic necessities. Unfortunately, the contracts do not provide extensive feminine job descriptions.[14]

Behind each of the formally notarized contracts recorded in Santiago lies a personal story of how indias and mestizas came to need jobs. Only in a few cases is part of the story told. For example, a mestiza named Ana, a little girl, was assigned to a ten-year contract in 1587.[15] Presumably, the arrangement was the feminine equivalent of the apprentice system used for boys who learned a trade from an employer.

Since Elvira, a thirteen-year-old Indian, was described as a troublemaker when she was put to work for two years in 1599, her contract was evidently designed as a punishment.[16] The Indian women, Isabel and Juana, who entered contracts with new employers in 1596 and 1597, complained that their former mistresses had mistreated them.[17] Brígida de Hoyo, a mestiza, obtained release from a contract because of physical abuse when she reported that her employers had her beaten as if she were an "india, or their slave." They had called in a magistrate who authorized the flogging and had her hair cut, a punishment Indians deeply resented. Her contract in 1599 had called for the curacy payment and a dress, two shifts, and shoes. When the corregidor annulled the agreement, he declared that Brígida should dress like a mestiza and give up the Indian-style clothing that she wore.[18] This Brígida, or another mestiza of the same name, was still wearing Indian apparel later in 1599 when she undertook a new two-year contract with better compensation consisting of two garments, the provision of food, medical care, and the curacy fee, plus bonuses of a grogram *faldellín* (full-length skirt) and shoes.[19]

Some employers were eager to re-hire female servants when a contract expired and thus maintain a permanent staff.[20] On the other hand, women with proven skills and an affinity for a particular household could demand better working conditions and greater compensation. For example, Juana, an Indian from Cuzco, agreed to work as a nursemaid for two years in 1588. In addition to her food, health care, and the stipend for the curacy, she would receive wages of ten gold pesos and a final bonus of three pairs of buttons.[21] In 1591, an india named Inés from Valdivia renewed her contract with Gonzalo de Toledo for two years to continue rearing his son. She explained that she had been treated well, Gonzalo now promised "to treat her like a free person," and she loved his little boy. As wages Inés would receive three garments annually.[22]

Contracts similar to these continued to be made in the Chilean cities and rural areas.[23] For example, documents dating from 1622 illustrate how the system operated while the Tasa de Esquilache was in effect. On October 6, Barbola, an Indian woman who was free rather than attached to an encomienda or enslaved, and her husband, a mulato slave named Francisco, apprenticed her son and his stepson, Juan, described as a mulato, to the Indian shoemaker, Francisco, for a three-year period. The shoemaker promised to teach the youth his trade, treat him well, and provide him annually with a pair of breeches, two shirts, and shoes. Since nothing was said about food or lodging, the Indian mother who wanted her son to become a craftsman apparently intended to continue to feed and house him until he could support himself. When the apprenticeship ended, final compensation from the shoemaker would consist of a suit of clothes with a cloak, two shirts, a jacket, and a hat. In return, Juan expressed his willingness to enter the contract, and his mother and stepfather pledged that the youth would continue to work for the shoemaker after the contract expired if he did not live up to his obligations. They also declared that they had permission from their master, Gaspar Hernández de la Serna, to apprentice Juan in this manner. The corregidor of Santiago, Pedro Lisperguer, then approved the contract which was witnessed by three men, one of whom signed for the shoemaker. It was notarized, for a fee of six reales, by Manuel de Toro Mazote, Gaspar's nephew.[24]

THE WORLD OF WORK

As the following abstract shows, the notary and his uncle were more directly involved when a high court judge hired out an Indian woman. The contract begins as follows:

"In the noble and very loyal city of Santiago, Chile, on September 20, 1622, before the gentleman licentiate Fernando Machado, of the council of His Majesty and his oidor in the royal audiencia of this kingdom, there appeared an Indian woman, who said her name was Luisa." She came of her own free will and wanted to make a contract to serve Doña Ana Félix Cifontes, the wife of Gaspar Hernández de la Serna, for the time of one year. She would work without failings or shortcomings.

After the oidor questioned her, Luisa stated that she was not under contract to any other person but had worked for Doña María Grajales, the wife of Jerónimo de Miranda, with whose consent she left that service. His grace, the oidor, approved the contract and set Luisa's wage for the year at twenty pesos, payable in clothing that she needed; she was also to receive good treatment. The notary then obliged himself to pay her if Gaspar Hernández did not do so and to give her lodging and ordinary food. Luisa formally repeated her promise to serve without faults, and if she failed, to continue to serve in the future. His grace commanded the india to serve and endorsed the contractual terms, provided that they did not prejudice any third parties. The witnesses were Pedro Rosa de Narváez, Pedro de Ariaga, and Gaspar Díaz Hidalgo. The manuscript bears only two signatures, that of the licentiate Machado and Manuel de Toro Mazote, who notarized it free of charge.[25]

The notary's generosity and willingness to underwrite the contract are partially explained by his kinship with Gaspar. Moreover, his wife, Juana Cifuentes (*sic*) Hidalgo was related to Ana Félix de Cifontes.[26]

These seventeenth-century legal instruments gave the employer significant leverage to extend the contractual work period. If the employee were considered guilty of failing, which presumably could include anything from unsatisfactory work to absenteeism, he or she was already obligated by the contract itself to continue in service after its expiration. From this it was only a small step to debt servitude. Indias and mestizas, nevertheless, contributed to the economic life of the colony through the contract system, harsh though it was.

Chapter 6
Beatriz Clara Coya:
Inca Princess and Chilean *Gobernadora*

The local village cacicas enjoyed certain advantages in the eyes of the law that set them above the workaday world of the india and mestiza commoner. However, even greater social differences separated the Chilean Indian leaders from the Inca royalty in neighboring Peru.[1] A hispanized member of that royal family was the most prestigious Indian woman to live in Chile during the period of Spanish rule. Although her biography pertains less directly to the history of Chile than to Peru, Beatriz Clara Coya and her mestiza daughter, Ana María Loyola y Coya, merit at least cursory attention here because they have attracted little notice outside the Latin world.

Beatriz Clara, whose title of Coya means princess in the Quechua language of the Andes, followed her husband Governor Martín García Oñez de Loyola to Chile, the land that her Inca forebears had only partially controlled. There the Araucanians, who had resisted her ancestors and whom the Spaniards never completely conquered, killed her husband in a surprise attack in 1598 that marked the beginning of an Indian offensive that did not abate until the Europeans were driven from their cities in the Araucanian country, leaving only Concepción and Castro as Spanish settlements in the south. Even a new outpost, which the governor had founded in Beatriz Clara's honor, was evacuated in 1599 as the Indian rebellion spread.[2]

According to the mestizo chronicler, Garcilaso de la Vega, known as "the Inca," Spaniards and Indians in Peru saw the governor's death as Indian vengeance for the execution of the famous Inca Túpac Amaru.[3] This interpretation carries more than a touch of irony as far as Beatriz Clara Coya is concerned because she was the widow of one and a relative of the other. She had been born in Peru to the Inca Sairi Túpac and his wife Cusi Huárcay, granddaughter of Emperor Huáscar. For a time, her father had governed the Inca rebel stronghold of Vilcabamba that his father, Manco Inca, had established. However, Sairi Túpac left the Andean retreat in 1557, came to terms with the Spaniards, accepted baptism with his wife, and took the name of Diego Sairi Túpac. The couple and their only child, Beatriz Clara, who was born about 1558, lived in a palace in Cuzco where her father had a large, valuable encomienda. Beatriz Clara was the heiress to the encomienda when he died in 1560. Meanwhile, her kinsmen ruled in Vilcabamba until Viceroy Francisco de Toledo sent Oñez de Loyola against the mountain kingdom in 1572. After Túpac Amaru fell prisoner, the young Inca was tried and executed in Cuzco.[4]

As a reward for capturing the Inca leader, Oñez de Loyala received a Peruvian encomienda.[5] Viceroy Toledo also arranged for him to marry Beatriz Clara Coya. Various civil and canonical questions postponed the wedding because another Spaniard claimed to be her husband, but the previous marriage which had taken place when she was a very young child between five and seven years of age, was finally annulled. Beatriz Clara Coya had evidently been coerced into the first marriage after being raped. There is some evidence that she had also been married to a cousin who died prior to her marriage to Oñez de Loyola.[6]

While their own marriage case was still in progress, Oñez de Loyola had hoped to return to Spain. He informed the crown that he wanted to bring Beatriz Clara Coya with him but needed more money for the trip and living expenses than his encomienda provided. In 1576 and 1577 Philip II issued two decrees awarding him another encomienda worth 1,000 pesos annually for two lives, his own and that of a successor, but imposed a number of conditions for him to obtain it. In the first place, when he left Peru, he would have to meet the usual requirement of appointing a squire to fulfill the military obligations of an encomendero. Secondly, Beatriz Clara could move to Spain only if she came of her own free will. Thirdly, her husband would begin to receive the revenue from the Indian tributes deposited in the royal treasury when they actually embarked from Peru. Finally, the departure had to be within three years.[7]

Viceroy Toledo formalized the writ of encomienda in 1578 with the stipulation that either one heir, a son or a daughter, or Oñez de Loyola's widow would inherit the encomienda. The income was to be held in the treasury until the couple sailed for Spain. If they did not go within three years, the encomienda would escheat to the crown.[8]

Beatriz Clara wrote a letter to her husband expressing her willingness to move to Spain, especially since she had lost some rights over the encomienda she had inherited from her father.[9] The time limit for departure soon expired, however, and the new encomienda was declared vacant. Oñez de Loyola then sought to regain it and used Beatriz Clara's letter as proof that she would go to Spain of her own free choice. He also argued that his political appointments in South America and complications arising from the marriage case had prevented them from meeting the departure deadline.[10]

The projected move to the peninsula became a moot question when Philip II named Oñez de Loyola governor and captain general of Chile in 1591. When he received this appointment, he petitioned for the right to inherit Beatriz Clara's own encomienda if she should die childless. He had already informed the crown that the authorities in Peru had treated them and her father unjustly. On the basis of her lineage and his own services, he thought they were entitled to her full paternal inheritance.[11]

Another more immediate problem for the *gobernadora* (governor's wife) and her husband was the fact that Viceroy Hurtado de Mendoza, himself a former Chilean governor, disapproved of the crown's new choice for the post. As a sign of his displeasure, he denied Oñez de Loyola permission to go to Cuzco for his wife.[12] The governor, therefore, proceeded to Chile alone and reached Santiago in October, 1592. Beatriz Clara arrived before the end of the year.[13]

The couple apparently lived in Concepción, and their daughter Ana María Loyola y Coya was born there.[14] However, they had some dealings in Santiago. For example, Beatriz Clara, as a widow, signed a document in 1599 promising to pay the protector of the Indians of Santiago for foodstuffs and other articles that Indian communities had furnished for the gubernatorial household.[15]

With her small daughter, the ex-gobernadora left Chile soon after her husband's death, and Viceroy Luis de Velasco notified the king on June 15, 1599, that they had arrived in Lima. Beatriz Clara's Peruvian encomienda, he asserted, was worth between 10,000 and 12,000 pesos annually, an ample dowry for Ana María to marry well.[16] This she did. Her husband was Juan Henríquez de Borja, the son of a marqués and the maternal grandson of the Duque de Gandía, Francisco Borja, who became a Jesuit after his wife died. Ana María's two sons could therefore claim as ancestors Inca royalty and a grandee of Spain, who was eventually canonized. Ana María and her descendants were also related to Ignatius Loyola, the founder of the Society of Jesus, because her father was his kinsman.[17]

Ana María herself made at least one formal plea to the crown for recognition of her rights as an Inca heiress.[18] Philip III granted her the title of marquesa de Oropesa, and she inherited a Peruvian encomienda from one of her parents. [19] Her son or grandson who obtained the Oropesa title claimed rights not only to the encomienda in Peru but also, because of the marquisate, some jurisdiction there.[20]

Ana María's wedding inspired one of the more famous paintings of the colonial period. It depicts the bride with young Borja, her Inca forebears, her parents, and the two Jesuit saints, Francisco Borja and Ignatius Loyola. The artistic work is symbolic of the continuing union between the peninsula and the Andes that the marriage of the daughter of an Inca princess and a Basque hidalgo had effected.[21]

Colonial chroniclers, in the main Jesuits, memorialized the marriages of Beatriz Clara Coya and Ana María to the peninsulars. Alonso de Ovalle and Diego de Rosales commented on the civic celebrations the Chileans had held in honor of the Inca gobernadora's arrival. Rosales added that as Governor Oñez de Loyola later made his rounds of the frontier he received letters from Beatriz Clara Coya entreating him to come to see her, but he continued on his military mission and soon met his death.[22] If she did write, this was probably her last communication with him. A contemporary praised the governor for placing duty before his wife and daughter;[23] perhaps the princess and ex-gobernadora with the melodious name and title found some comfort in his reputation during her widowhood. Regrettably, her personal reactions to her experiences as First Lady of the southern kingdom, if ever recorded, have yet to be discovered.

Beatriz Clara Coya was the first and last Indian gobernadora in Chile. After her husband's death, his successors in the governorship would continue to adminster the realm in the name of the king for another two centuries. The colony gradually matured, not always in the sense of discernible upward progress, but rather in terms of the modification of culture and customs. Women from the several racial groups and social levels were, as we have seen, both active and passive agents helping to effect these changes.

Conclusion

The evidence compiled in this monograph on the nonwhite female experience in colonial Chile is perhaps most significant from the standpoint of the diversity of that experience. No thoroughly typical woman emerges from the complex and often contradictory data. While many women faced analogous circumstances, each female had a unique personality and made her own contributions, all too often anonymously and frequently passively, to the development of the colony. The unnamed African and Araucanian remembered primarily as ciphers in the account book of a slaver or the report of a government inspector had little in common with an Inca princess-gobernadora and defy simple generalizations. It is appropriate therefore to review the collective experience of nonwhite women with reference to the contrasts that characterized their lives.

The active roles that females assumed in colonial times are readily discernible in the text and need scant summation. Blacks, Indians, and mixed bloods who sued in the courts to defend their rights and petitioned the authorities to obtain redress of grievances quite obviously demonstrated personal initiative in a society that did little to encourage such female assertiveness. The documentation on economic pursuits reveals a broad spectrum of productive endeavors. Some of the more important include ownership and management of real property, usually, it is true, small holdings; craft enterprises, especially spinning, weaving and tailoring; retail sales; health services; child care and instruction; household maintenance, food preparation, laundry services; animal husbandry; other chores on ranches and farms; and at times exhausting manual labor. Participants in religious celebrations were actively engaged in a distinctive cultural phenomenon. Since most nonwhites had limited options open to them, the fact that so many individuals seized opportunities to improve their legal status, living conditions, and socio-cultural environment is a telling commentary on their innate ability to profit from adversity.

Church and state did, of course, render assistance and encouragement to Negroid, Indian, and mestiza women. These positive features of the law and religion served as buffers against the dehumanizing milieu in which all but a few lived. The measures offered reassurance of human worth.

Pronouncements by Church and State demanding respect for nonwhite Chileans as persons and protection for their spiritual and physical well-being were part of the larger campaign for social justice in Spanish America and reaffirmed Bartolomé de las Casas' conviction that all the peoples of the world are full members of the human race.[1] Its few successes and many failures so soon become familiar to Latin Americanists that the campaign itself can be underestimated. Such routine enjoinders as those requiring employers to provide contractual workers with medical care and food take on heightened significance in the light of the persistent problems of illness and malnutrition in the contemporary world.

While well-intentioned clergymen and officials sought to defend basic rights and to ameliorate blatant injustices, Chile, like other Spanish colonies, continued to manifest not only restraints and repression but also discriminatory racial attitudes. General legislation applicable to nonwhite groups aimed at controlling behavior thought to be disruptive to society. Royal decrees, gubernatorial orders, and municipal ordinances reiterated proscriptions and penalties with distressing monotony. As Magnus Mörner has remarked, "leaders of government obviously were imbued with the same prejudice as others . . . "[2] State and Church countenanced bondage, and neither issued an ipso facto condemnation of Negroid slavery nor conducted an effective campaign against racial prejudice.

Racial slurs punctuated official and private papers from the era of conquest to the eve of independence. Chilean actuality nevertheless belied the stereotypes portrayed in contemporary records. In analyzing the place of blacks in Peruvian conquest society, James Lockhart found that while black people "were subordinated to Spaniards," they "counted as individuals."[3] This paradox finds an analogy in the condition of nonwhite women in colonial Chile. Examples of law-abiding workers contradict the criticism regularly leveled against nonwhites as being prone to laziness, crime, and alcoholism. Whites themselves occasionally recognized and rewarded individual women in their wills, thereby acknowledging the inaccuracy of the stereotypes. In the early years, affluence was measured in terms of the size of an encomienda. Throughout the colonial period, Afro-Chilean slaves were assigned monetary values indicative of their importance in the Chilean labor pool and as capital assets in private fortunes. Lobbying to legalize Indian slavery and financial outlays to acquire Negroid slaves demonstrate that the prospective slave owners expected to profit from the endeavors of bondswomen. Similarly, labor contracts show that employers were eager to hire nonwhite women. The laws mandating contractual labor for the unemployed reflected the prevailing attitude of Spaniards in Spain and in America who assumed that persons of inferior social status should work. Elitist concepts and race prejudice thus existed side-by-side with awareness of the contributions female nonwhite commoners were making.

The amount of legislation defining the status of indias far outweighs the attention given to black and mixed blood females. This was true throughout Spanish America because the Indian was believed to have special rights and to constitute a separate commonwealth (república). Moreover, indias who remained in their villages and those who wore their traditional dress in cities and on Spanish landholdings were easily identifiable as subjects of legislation. At the same time, Spain had no single Indian policy applicable to all Amerindians. Instead, general legislation established ground rules that admitted of exceptions. Since particularism characterized so much of colonial law, it was natural for a corpus of special legislation to emerge in response to specific situations that arose from contacts between Spaniards and Indians. Chile itself was a special case. The large numbers of unpacified Indians in the south, the debates on the Araucanian war, and the military conflict itself all demanded official notice, and the law accordingly mentioned both males and females. This fact is underscored by the special section devoted to Chilean Indians in the Recopilación. Book VI, title 16 of the code differentiates them from each other in classifications stipulating place of residence, occupation, age, marital status, and sex.

Similar features are apparent in regard to Negroid slavery and the status of free blacks, mulatas, and zambas. The law embodied general precepts that could be and were modified not only by particular legislative enactments but also by judicial verdicts and injunctions that had the force of law.

As the colonial period drew to a close, racial designations continued to denote parentage and pigmentation. The eighteenth-century historian Felipe Gómez de Vidaurre, for example, divided the Chileans into three basic groups — white, Indian, and black — plus multiple castes derived from race mixture, including the mestizo, mulato, and zambo elements.[4] The historical record on these racially mixed individuals is nevertheless ambiguous because as their numbers

CONCLUSION

increased they evidently attracted less official attention. There were several reasons for this. Precedents established earlier through law and custom remained in effect and required little elaboration. Both informal sexual unions and interracial marriages blessed by the Church did much to facilitate, as William F. Sater has noted, the absorption of blacks into the populace at large.[5] Persons of Euro-Indian lineage also joined "white" society. As better documentation on the pervasive process of *mestizaje* (race mixture) becomes available, social mobility can be charted more precisely. This in turn will permit a more accurate assessment of the nexus between being female and the question of race and class.

In her study of sixteenth-century Indian women in Arequipa, Peru, Elinor C. Burkett suggests that females were more readily assimilated into Spanish culture than males in the early colonial period because of their close associations with the Europeans.[6] A similar analysis of the status of nonwhite men and women from the same social and economic peer groups in colonial Chile might produce comparable results.

Answers to the most elementary questions regarding Chilean colonial demography are among the most elusive of those awaiting further research. Even the better recent studies do not always distinguish between the numbers of males and females. This is understandable because, as previously explained, serious problems hamper scholars engaged in statistical work. Despite these obstacles, a variety of valid archival projects present a monumental but exciting challenge to young historians, particularly Chileans. The range and complexity of the unanswered questions mean that the work will require teams of investigators or at least coordinated efforts to uncover the archival secrets. A group of Chilean scholars has recently undertaken a demographic study of elite families in Santiago from 1750 to 1880 which might serve as a model for others focusing on the middle and lower sectors of society during the colonial centuries.[7] Localities other than Santiago and the Central Valley should, of course, come under scrutiny.

Topics that invite further analysis include several pertaining to Afro-Chileans. The slave trade should be investigated in order to refine the estimates of the numbers of blacks imported and to obtain data on their age, sex, and African origins. Statistics should also be compiled on the internal slave trade, taking note of the traffic in bozales and Chilean-born blacks, mulatos and mulatas, zambos and zambas. Since bills of sale described the slaves and sometimes

71

mentioned health and skills, the research will divulge more than a scale of prices and thus expand upon the kind of preliminary data available in general histories.[8] Numerical tabulations of deeds of manumission during the early, middle, and later periods of Spanish rule would also be instructive, especially if the reasons for seeking and granting freedom are cataloged. Both Negroid and Indian slaves figured in marital endowments and the appraisals of posthumous estates; quantitative studies should therefore compare the monetary value assigned to them with that of other property.

If sufficient documentation can be located, it might be possible to learn what legal status devolved upon the children born to enslaved Araucanians. Notarial registries might contain clues to their employment. Those sources, as indicated in the text, mention working women and should be inventoried to yield a fuller occupational index than is currently available.

Thoroughgoing histories of Chilean nunneries have not yet materialized. Intensive investigations of the convents will no doubt reveal significant data on their servants and slaves and the incidence of nonwhite religious aspirants becoming nuns.

Until more research is done, definitive conclusions about the dimensions and nuances of the nonwhite female experience must be withheld. This preliminary study nevertheless discloses that women of African and Indian descent were essential, usually exploited, elements in the colony. Occasionally an exceptional woman overcame impediments to advancement. A few outstanding females accommodated themselves to Hispanic society, at whatever unknown cost to themselves and their traditional culture, and were admitted, if not welcomed, into elite circles. Together Afro-Chilean, Indian, and mestiza women added not a page but chapters filled with human drama to the history of the far southern realm.

Glossary

Acequia. Canal.

Alguacil mayor. Ex officio city councilman holding the post of chief constable and as such empowered to appoint deputies.

Arras. Groom's wedding gift to the bride.

Audiencia. High court of justice with some administrative and legislative functions.

Auto. Executive order, decree, or edict.

Blanca, blanco. Female, male white.

Bozales. Black slaves recently arrived from Africa.

Cabildo. Municipal council.

Cacica. Indian headwoman.

Cacique. Indian headman.

Cartas, or *papeles, de venta.* Letters of sale. Legal documents authorizing the sale of a slave to a new owner.

Castellano. The gold *peso* of the sixteenth century.

Cédula real. Royal order or decree.

Chácaras, chacras. Small farms on the outskirts of a city.

Cofradía. Religious confraternity that performed mutual aid functions.

Conquistadora. Female conqueror.

Corregidor. Provincial administrative and judicial official; presiding officer of the *cabildo* in principal cities; some *corregidores* exercised jurisdiction over Indians.

Criolla, criollo. American-born female, male offspring of Spanish parents.

Cuadra. A city block; also a unit of rural land measure.

Don, Doña. Masculine, feminine title of respect.

Encomendera, encomendero. Female, male recipient of a grant of Indians.

Encomienda. Grant of Indians, primarily as tributaries.

Estancia. Large rural landholding; not always devoted exclusively to ranching.

Faldellín. Woman's full-length overskirt.

Fiscal. Crown attorney attached to an *audiencia,* similar to an attorney general.

Gobernadora. Wife of a governor (*gobernador*).

Hacienda. Large rural landholding.

India, indio. Female, male Indian.

Ladina, ladino. Hispanized Negroid female, male.

Lusitana. Portuguese female.

Maloca. Invasion of Indian lands for purposes of capturing and enslaving the natives; slave hunt.

Mayorazgo. Entailed estate.

Mesada. Tax on certain offices.

Mestiza, mestizo. Female, male Euro-Indian.

Mestizaje. Racial mixture; miscegenation.

Mulata, mulato. Female, male Euro-African.

Negra, negro. Female, male full-blooded black.

Oidor. High court judge; minister of an *audiencia.*

Peninsular. Spaniard born in Spain but living in America.

Peso. The Spanish piece of eight composed of eight silver *reales* (*peso de plata*). The *peso de oro* was the gold *peso* also called the *castellano* in the sixteenth century.

Poseedora. Mistress, female owner.

Presidente. Presiding judge in an *audiencia;* the office pertained to the governor of Chile while the *audiencia* of Concepción functioned in the sixteenth century and after the high court of Santiago was inaugurated in 1609; unless he was a school-trained lawyer, the governor could not, however, vote on cases of a strictly judicial nature.

Pueblo. Village, especially of Indians.

Pulperías. Retail shops selling wine and staples.

Real. The eighth part of a silver *peso.*

República. Commonwealth.

Residencia. Judicial review of an official's term of office.

Tasa. Tribute assessment.

Yanaconas. Male and female Indian servitors permanently attached to a household.

Zamba, zambo. Female, male Afro-Indian.

Abbreviations

The following abbreviations are used in the notes and bibliography:

AAS	Archivo del Arzobispado de Santiago.
BACH	*Boletín de la academia chilena de la historia.*
BHC	*Biblioteca hispano-chilena* (Medina).
DAAS	*Colección de documentos* (Lizana and Maulén).
DI, 1st ser.	*Colección de documentos inéditos,* 1st ser. (Medina).
DI, 2nd ser.	*Colección de documentos inéditos,* 2nd ser. (Medina).
ES	Chile, Archivo Nacional, Archivo de los escribanos de Santiago.
HAHR	*Hispanic American Historical Review.*
Historiadores	*Colección de historiadores* (Medina and others).
RCHG	*Revista chilena de historia y geografía.*
RLRI	*Recopilación de leyes de los reynos de las Indias.*
TAm	*The Americas: A Quarterly Review of Inter-American Cultural History.*

Notes

(Complete authors' names, titles, and publication data are given in the Bibliography.)

Introduction

[1] Eyzaguirre, *Historia,* the best single volume on colonial Chile, proved particularly helpful in preparing these introductory remarks. Loveman, 9-115, provides a useful summary of colonial times in English.
[2] Rout, xv, 210, 212.

Part I:
Afro-Chilean Women

[1] "Codicilo del gobernador don Diego de Almagro," Cuzco, July 8, 1538, transcribed from a copy made in Cuzco, Jan. 31, 1539, in *DI,* 1st ser., V, 218-227; Vial Correa, *Africano,* 15, 176; Bowser, "Colonial Spanish America," 20-21 and note 3. Bowser adds in *The African Slave,* 7-8, 356 note 23, that Margarita made a loan to the royal treasury to help suppress the Girón rebellion in 1554. A summary transcript of the "Deed of Emancipation," issued in Lima, May 8, 1539, is in Clemence, 97.
[2] Errázuriz, *Chile sin gobernador,* 89-90, includes the quotation. On Juan Valiente and Juana Valdivia see also Boyd-Bowman, 150-151; Vial Correa, *Africano,* 15-16, 19-20, 174-176; Sater, 16; Bowser, "Colonial Spanish America," 20; Rout, 75-77; Thayer Ojeda, *Formación,* III, 320-323; Medina, *Diccionario,* 930; Roa y Ursúa, 122; Anon., "Memoria de los vecinos de Chile á quien Francisco de

Villagra despojó de sus indios," in *Historiadores,* XXIX, 509-510.
³The bill of sale is in Avila Martel and Bravo Lira, 174-175. See Thayer Ojeda, *Santiago urbana,* 126, on Agustín Briceño and his mestiza wife, Francisca de Tarabajano.
⁴"Información de los méritos y servicios de Alonso de Córdoba," 1549, in *DI,* 1st ser., VIII, 454-491; Vial Correa, *Africano,* 18-19; Espejo, *Nobiliario,* 277-278. Bermúdez Plata, III, 145, lists a party of twelve persons including servants, but the term slave is not used.
⁵"Instrucción dada por el virrey García Hurtado de Mendoza al almirante Hernando Lamero para su viaje a Chile en guarda de la costa contra los corsarios," 1591, in *DI,* 2nd ser., IV, 129-137.
⁶Thayer Ojeda, "Apuntes," 195.
⁷Curtin, 89, Table 24; Sater, 17-22; Vial Correa, *Africano,* 68-81; Mellafe, *Esclavitud,* 91, and his *Esclavitud negra en Chile,* can be supplemented by data on the Chilean slave trade in Rout, 27-75.

Chapter 1,
Law and Religion

¹Davis, 224-225 note 1, offers a useful synopsis and criticism of Tannenbaum's *Slave and Citizen: The Negro in the Americas* (New York, 1947).
²Discussions of peninsular and colonial legislation include Davis, 165-173, 223-243, and *passim;* Bowser, "Colonial Spanish America," 19-36, 38-42; Rout, 80-87; Mörner, 35-48, 111-125. The several editions of *Las Siete Partidas* include an English version, tr. Samuel Parsons Scott; the code treats slavery in several places, especially *Partida* IV, titles XXI-XXII, and XXIII, prologue, laws 1-2.
³*Actas,* I, 272-273 (1551: July 31); Sater, 28-29. *RLRI,* Book VII, title V, law 12, is a similar decree first issued in 1542.
⁴Santiago city ordinances, March 30, 1569, in Gay, I, 201; Sater, 29; Barros Arana, III, 128; Vial Correa, *Africano,* 131. Compare with "Bando" of Governor Juan Henríquez, Santiago, April 6, 1672, in *Actas,* XXXVIII, 217-218.
⁵Santiago city ordinances, March 30, 1569, in Gay, I, 196.
⁶*Ibid.,* 202; see *RLRI,* Book VII, title V, law 7, for a similar decree first issued in 1551.
⁷Santigao city ordinances, March 30, 1569, in Gay, I, 197-199; Vial

Correa, *Africano,* 131.

[8]*RLRI,* Book VII, title V, and Solórzano y Pereyra, Book II, chap. XXX, provide various examples. See also Sater, 28-33; Rout, 80-87, 99-104, 126-161, 329-330; Davis, 223-243.

[9]"Ordenanzas dictadas por el licenciado Melchor [*sic*] Calderón para los negros del reino de Chile," Santiago, Nov. 10, 1577, in *DI,* 2nd ser., II, 336-339. Vial Correa, *Africano,* 145-146; Sater, 30-31; Barros Arana, III, 128-129 and note 10. It was probably Gonzalo Calderón rather than Melchor who drafted these ordinances; on the two men see *ibid.,* II, 441, 448, 453, 459, III, 13-14 and note 10, 140; Briseño, 114, 194; Thayer Ojeda, *Santiago urbana,* 130; Bermúdez Plata, III, 150-156; Roa y Ursúa, 280, 288, 422.

[10]*Actas,* XXXI, 227-228 (1637: March 3); Vial Correa, *Africano,* 168; Sater, 46 note 71.

[11]*Ibid.,* 29-31; Vial Correa, *Africano,* 132-134; Amunátegui, 406-408. Rout, 99-125, treats revolts and resistance with some Chilean examples.

[12]*Actas,* XXVIII, 354, 360 (1626: Feb. 17, March 3); XLIII, 307-308 (1695: Oct. 29); Flusche, "Councilmen and Export Policies," 494-495.

[13]*Actas,* XXXIII, 130-131 (1646: Oct. 19); Barros Arana, IV, 418-419 and note 11.

[14]"R.C. prohibiendo la saca de esclavos negros y la esclavitud de las chinas," Madrid, Dec. 13, 1648, in Konetzke, II, 438-439. As the title indicates, this same decree mentioned Mujica's ordinance concerning the young female servitors known as *chinas.*

[15]Perhaps the most famous example of the sale of Afro-Chileans in Peru concerns the slaves who had formerly belonged to the expelled Society of Jesus. See Amunátegui Solar, *Historia social de Chile,* 186-187.

[16]Examples are *Actas,* XXIV, 181, 183, 209-210, 277-279, 283, 285 (1610: July 9, 23; 1611: Jan. 5; Sept. 13, 16, 23, 30); XXX, 13 (1628: April 28). See also Flusche, "Public Health," 173-176; Sater, 32. *RLRI,* Book VI, title I, laws 36, 38, and title XVI, law 63, pertain to Indian alcoholism.

[17]Auto of Governor Francisco Lazo de la Vega, Santiago, March 6, 1635, in *Actas,* XXXI, 84-87.

[18]*Ibid.,* XXXVI, 265-328 (1664: March 21), contains the fiscal's arguments and the testimony presented as the audiencia decided to sell a new office of *fiel ejecutor* between 1659 and 1664. See also Medina, *Cosas,* 262-263, and Flusche, "Public Health," 174-175. Muñoz was promoted to oidor in 1662 and died in office in 1667; his widow, Ana

Flores, was a slave owner. Silva i Molina, 50-52; Roa y Ursúa, 677-678, 696.

[19]Examples are "Ordenanzas acerca de la orden que se ha de tener en el tratamiento con los negros para la conservación de la política que han de tener," *ca.* 1545, in Konetzke, I, 237-240, and "Real instrucción sobre la educación, trato y ocupación de los esclavos," Aranjuez, May 31, 1789, in *ibid.,* III, 643-652.

[20]*RLRI,* Book VII, title V, law 28.

[21]*Actas,* XXX, 288-293 (1631: Oct. 17, 23); the first of these sessions is a *cabildo abierto* which prominent individuals attended; see also Vial Correa, *Africano,* 127; Sater, 32, 47 note 84.

[22]"Real cédula en que se ordena que los negros y negras de las Indias anden vestidos," Madrid, Dec. 2, 1672, in *DAAS,* III, 612-614.

[23]*Ibid.*

[24]*Ibid.*

[25]"Real cédula sobre que no se permita que salgan de noche de las casas de sus dueños las negras esclavas ni libres," Madrid, Dec. 2, 1672, in *DAAS,* III, 614-616; see also Vial Correa, *Africano,* 140.

[26] "Real cédula para que los gobernadores y justicias de las Indias no consientan que en los esclavos ejecuten sus dueños excesos ni crueldades ni que las esclavas anden desnudas," Madrid, April 19, 1710, in *DAAS,* IV, 209-210.

[27]*Partidas,* Partida IV, title XXII, law 4.

[28]"Real instrucción sobre la educación, trato y ocupación de los esclavos," Aranjuez, May 31, 1789, in Konetzke, III, 643-652, and "Consulta del Consejo de las Indias sobre el reglamento expedido en 31 de mayo de 1789 para la mejor educación, buen trato y ocupación de los negros esclavos de América," Madrid, March 17, 1794, in *ibid.,* III, 726-732; Vial Correa, *Africano,* 140-143; Rout, 82-87.

[29]Medina, *Cosas,* 261-262.

[30]"Instrucción," in Konetzke, III, 647-649; Rout, 83-84.

[31]Vial Correa, *Africano,* 147.

[32]"Visita a los oficiales reales de Mendoza y San Juan y cargos contra el corregidor de la provincia de Cuyo, d. Juan de la Banda," 1678-1679, in Espejo, *Cuyo,* I, 270-278. See also "Cartas a la real audiencia sobre la conducta de d. Juan de la Banda, corregidor de Cuyo en información hecha en San Luis sobre la misma materia," 1678, in *ibid.,* 265-268.

[33]Vial Correa, *Africano,* 147-148.

[34]*Ibid.,* 148; Medina, *Cosas,* 80-81; Sater, 34-35; Díaz Meza, VIII, 193-197.

[35]Data can be found in Letters of Bishops Francisco de Salcedo and Diego de Humanzoro to the king, Santiago, 1633-1634, 1669, in *DAAS,* I, 157-172, 295; [Huerta Gutiérrez], "Informe," La Ligua, May 31, 1660 and San Lorenzo, June 3, 1660, 133-141; Amunátegui Solar, *Encomiendas,* II, 121-160, "Apuntaciones," 73-75, "Documentos," 159-179; Boxer, 45-48; Vial Correa, *Africano,* 144.

[36]*Ibid.,* 148-150.

[37]*Partidas,* Partida IV, title XXI, law 6; Vial Correa, *Africano,* 150-151, 162; Molina, II, 324-325; Davis, 102-103.

[38]Vial Correa, *Africano,* 49.

[39]*Ibid.,* 155-156.

[40]*Ibid.,* 150-157; Sater, 34-35.

[41]Vial Correa, *Africano,* 162-166; Rout, 88-90; Bowser, "Colonial Spanish America," 19-36; *Partidas,* Partida III, title II, law 8; Partida IV, title XXII; Partida V, title V, law 45.

[42]Rout, 89; Bowser, "Colonial Spanish America," 23-24.

[43]Antonio complained that Rodrigo de Quiroga had been too indebted to free the slave himself, "Informe presentado en el Consejo de Indias sobre una solicitud de don Antonio de Quiroga para que se la conceda el hábito de la orden de Santiago," Madrid, Dec. 20, 1590, in *DI,* 2nd ser., VI, 319-322; Quiroga, "Memoria," in *Historiadores,* XXIX, 436-440. "Párrafos del testamento de Rodrigo de Quiroga, " Santiago, Feb. 24, 1580, in *DI,* 2nd ser., II, 474-477, does not include the clause on manumission.

[44]Vial Correa, *Africano,* 163.

[45]Amunátegui Reyes, I, 47-50, 105-106; the notary's posthumous inventory in 1770 listed nine slaves, *ibid.,* 63-69.

[46]Posthumous will of don Tomás de Azúa e Iturgoyen written by his widow, Santiago, Dec. 17, 1757, in Amunátegui Solar, *Mayorazgos,* III, 263-270. The will and the family are discussed in *ibid.,* 135-209. María Constanza's husband was her maternal uncle; they had an ecclesiastical dispensation for the marriage. She was pregnant with her husband's posthumous child when she wrote the will and took care to include the unborn heir with the three other children. *Leyes de Toro,* laws 31-39, pertain to the use of a power of attorney to write the will of another party.

[47]"Instrucción," in Konetzke, III, 647; Bowser, "Colonial Spanish America," 23; Rout, 88.

[48]Molina, II, 324-325; Vial Correa, *Africano,* 166-167, 170; Bowser, "Colonial Spanish America," 24-36; Rout, 87-93; *Partidas,* Partida III, title II, law 8; Partida IV, title XXII; *RLRI,* Book VII, title V, law

6.

[49]Vial Correa, *Africano,* 166.

[50]ES, vol. 89, protocols of Manuel de Toro Mazote, f 144v. The notary was Elena de la Serna's son, who notarized the document free of charge; Thayer Ojeda, *Santiago urbana,* 226-227, gives the relationship.

[51]Vial Correa, *Africano,* 170-171.

[52]*Partidas,* Partida IV, title XVII, law 8; *The Visigothic Code,* Book V, title IV, law 12; see also the editor's comment in the latter, 164 note 1.

[53]"Pragmática sanción para evitar el abuso de contraer matrimonios desiguales," El Pardo, March 23, 1776, and royal decree applying the pragmatic sanction to the Indies, El Pardo, April 7, 1778, in Konetzke, III, 406-413, 438-442; Vial Correa, "Prejuicios sociales," 17-29, and his "Aplicación de la pragmática," 319-334; Guarda Geywitz, 180-183; Rout, 141-142.

[54]Examples are "Ordenanzas acerca de la orden que se ha de tener en el tratamiento con los negros para la conservación de la política que han de tener," *ca.* 1545, in Konetzke, I, 237-240, and "R.C. que las audiencias y gobernadores pongan muy particular cuidado en el buen tratamiento de los esclavos," Buen Retiro, Oct. 13, 1683, in *ibid.,* II, 754; see also Rout, 81, 135-140.

[55]Vial Correa, *Africano,* 109-118. Medina, *Cosas,* 233-236, mentions a decree that Bishop Humanzoro issued on Jan. 7, 1667, threatening Indians and blacks with excommunication and forty lashes if they failed to receive the sacraments during Lent. *Synodo diocesana, que celebró el ilustrísimo señor doctor don Manuel de Alday y Aspee, obispo de Santiago de Chile, 1763,* Title XIX, constitution III, mentions blacks and mulatos and the observance of feast days.

[56]Eyzaguirre, *Historia,* 174; Vial Correa, *Africano,* 112-114.

[57]Ovalle, 186-188, 360-366.

[58]*Ibid.,* 366-368. When there is doubt about the validity or the fact of a previous baptism, Church law permits a person to be baptized conditionally. In such cases, the formula of baptism is prefaced by the words: "if you are not already baptized."

[59]*Ibid.,* 368.

[60]*Ibid.,* 360-368. One might also speculate that the author, who wrote his chronicle while in Europe seeking recruits for the apostolate in Chile, wanted to encourage members of his order to embrace the life of self-denial that service among the poor in Chile involved.

⁶¹Vial Correa, *Africano,* 109-111; Medina, *Cosas,* 195; Thayer Ojeda, *Santiago urbana,* 74, 193; Rout, 135.

⁶²Information against bachiller Rodrigo González, Lima, Oct. 6, 1556, in *DI,* 1st ser., XXVIII, 57-68, 111-112; Vial Correa, *Africano,* 16-17, 57 note 1, 174; Roa y Ursúa, 65. Errázuriz, *Chile sin gobernador,* 427-460, finds some of the charges and testimony concerning González Marmolejo specious.

⁶³Testimony of Bernardino de Mella, Lima, Oct. 30, 1548, in *DI,* 1st ser., VIII, 295-300.

⁶⁴Amunátegui Solar, "Trata," 36; Vial Correa, *Africano,* 121-122.

⁶⁵*Synodo 1763,* Title VIII, constitution XIV.

⁶⁶*Synodo 1688,* Chap. IX, constitution VI.

⁶⁷Medina, *Inquisición,* I, 269-270, 272-273, 277-278, 339, II, 268.

⁶⁸*Ibid.,* I, 406-408; Vial Correa, *Africano,* 118; Rout, 137.

⁶⁹Medina, *Inquisición,* II, 493-494, citing Pedro de Peralta Barnuevo, *Triunfos del santo oficio peruano;* Rout, 137; Vial Correa, *Africano,* 119.

⁷⁰*Ibid.,* 137.

Chapter 2,
The Economy

¹Vial Correa, *Africano,* 158-161; Davis, 224-225 and note 1; Medina, *Cosas,* 195, Errázuriz, *García de Mendoza,* 60-61 note 1; Vicuña Mackenna, I, 352 note 1. Rout, 69-75, 323-328, includes data on Chile.

²Sater, 17-22.

³Amunátegui Solar, *Mayorazgos,* II, 65-186.

⁴Examples of Alonso del Campo's business dealings and bureaucratic career are ES, vol. 89, protocols of Manuel de Toro Mazote, fs 105, 113-114, 140-141v, 164-165v; *Actas,* XX, 407-413 (1592: Nov. 11), XXX, 376-377 (1632: Oct. 22); Thayer Ojeda, *Santiago urbana,* 59, 61-62, 90, 98, 101; Góngora, *Encomenderos,* 94-95, and his "Social Stratification," 436-441.

⁵ES, vol. 89, protocols of Manuel de Toro Mazote, fs 93-96v, 190v-191, Dowry Promise and Dowry Receipt for Magdalena del Campo Lantadilla and Business Contract of Fernando Bravo [de Naveda] and

Juan Cajal, Feb. 20, 1623. The registry does not include Juan Cajal's memorandum.

[6]*Ibid.*, fs 134-134v, 140-140v, 142v, 143, 144v, 164-165v, 166v-167, 191v-192, 194-194v.

[7]*Ibid.*, and Avila Martel and Bravo Lira, 171-175.

[8]Amunátegui Solar, *Mayorazgos*, I, 14-22, "Carta de dote de María de Torres," Santiago, Jan. 30, 1686, 49-58; see also Barbier, 421, 426; Vial Correa, *Africano*, 37-38; Díaz Meza, VII, 274-277, X, 127-129.

[9]"Memoria de las cosas que dan en casamiento el señor Pedro de Astorga," in *Actas*, XXXI, 146-148, following minutes of the Oct. 26, 1635, session. The cabildo notary Manuel de Toro Mazote complained that he needed a new book for the council minutes, and the next session authorized the purchase of a new volume for the records, *ibid.*, 148 (1635: Oct. 28); since he was running out of paper, Manuel apparently jotted down the information on the dowry on the last pages of the old book. Roa y Ursúa, 552-553; Thayer Ojeda, *Santiago urbana*, 120, identify the bride and groom.

[10]Amunátegui Solar, *Mayorazgos*, III, 341-372, 413-415, "Testamento de don Manuel Calvo de Encalada i Chacón," Santiago, Sept. 16, 1795, 401-408. Manuel's mother, Catalina Chacón y Carvajal, the first marquesa de Villapalma, as noted previously, served as custodian of a slave woman in 1709. She descended from Magdalena del Campo Lantadilla. Her granddaughters María Teresa and María Antonia Encalada y Recabarren respectively married the audiencia ministers, José de Gorbea y Vadillo and Fernando Márquez de la Plata. On their husbands, see Lohmann Villena, 51-52, 64-65; Burkholder and Chandler, *passim*. Marquez de la Plata, 92, comments on María Antonia's personal property.

[11]ES, vol. 772, protocols of Luis Luque de Moreno, fs 243-284v. A partial list of Inés' assets is in Amunátegui Reyes, I, 50-57.

[12]ES, vol. 87, protocols of Manuel de Toro Mazote, fs 28-38v. Amunátegui Solar, *Mayorazgos*, I, 231-329, collects data, including documents, on Isabel Osorio de Cáceres, the Bravo de Saravia family, and its merger with a branch of the Irarrázaval family.

[13]Lorenza, whose roots lay in the south where her father had a distinguished military career encompassing the second half of the sixteenth century, was the daughter of Lorenzo Bernal de Mercado and María de Rojas Pliego. Medina edited and published a version of Juan de Mendoza Monteagudo's *Las guerras de Chile: poema histórico*, with documentary appendices reproducing the testamentary provisions and inventory studied here. The will in *ibid.*, 263, 267,

mentioned that Lorenza had a dowry worth approximately 4,000 pesos plus an income of 900 pesos that the crown assigned her from Peruvian sources. For genealogical information, see Thayer Ojeda, "La familia del conquistador Juan de Cuevas," 157-158, and *Santiago urbana,* 171-172; Roa y Ursúa, 25, 43-44, 107-109, 154; Espejo, *Nobiliario,* 350-357, 492-493.

[14]The will in Mendoza Monteagudo, 255-274, incorporates the powers of attorney and Juan's testamentary *memorias;* the inventory is 275-277.

[15]Powers of attorney and will, in *ibid.,* 256, 259, 261, 264-265, 267, 271-272. To bequeath a joint conjugal estate to illegitimate offspring was rare; more typical was Juan's recognition of the natural sons and the small bequest, drawn from the Peruvian income.

[16]Power of attorney of Lorenza Bernal de Mercado, in *ibid.,* 261-262.

[17]Will and inventory, in *ibid.,* 264, 270-271, 275-276. The audiencia played some role in guaranteeing Alonso's freedom.

[18]The data on María de Mendoza's slave woman and other aspects of her estate appear in *ibid.,* 266, 268-269, 271-274.

[19]Will and inventory, in *ibid.,* 263-264, 270, 275-276. Petrona's selling price was listed at 450 pesos in the will and 556 in the inventory. The niece was Inés de Zárate.

[20]Amunátegui Solar, *Mayorazgos,* I, 268-270, 322-333, "Emancipación de don Miguel de Irarrázaval i Bravo de Saravia," Santiago, Oct. 2, 1728, 363-368. Miguel, aged twenty-two, was released from paternal authority by his father and received the maternal and paternal necessary inheritance from both parents.

[21]*Ibid.,* 329-333, "Institución del mayorazgo Irarrázaval," Santiago, Oct. 2, 1728, 355-363.

[22]*Ibid.,* II, 1-18, "Institución del mayorazgo Aguirre," Santiago, Oct. 12, 1744, 55-64; Vial Correa, *Africano,* 161. This family is distinct from that of the conquistador Francisco de Aguirre. Juan Nicolás obtained the marquisate of Montepío in 1755. He sold the estancia destined for the entail; the land, but not the slaves, was regained from the purchaser. Juan Nicolás' second wife, Antonia Balbontín de la Torre, claimed that he and Ignacia Díaz wanted to revoke the entire mayorazgo.

[23]Amunátegui Solar, *Mayorazgos,* III, 23-29, "Institución del mayorazgo Toro Zambrano," Santiago, April 3, 1789, 56-87.

[24]*Ibid.,* 41 and note 1; Eyzaguirre, *Conde,* 208, 212 note 4.

[25]ES, vol. 898, protocols of Tadeo Gómez de Silva, fs 174-176;

Amunátegui Solar, *Mayorazgos,* III, 18-22, 53-56; Eyzaguirre, *Conde,* 70-72, 76 note 12, 134, 139-140, 148, 155. María Josefa de Toro Zambrano y Váldes was with her husband in Peru when the Túpac Amaru II revolt began. She tried to use a slave woman to obtain things she needed, but her agent sold the black woman for 400 pesos and absconded with the money, *ibid.,* 133-139, 166-167 notes 15-19; Florez Vicuña, 159-162.

[26]Vicuña Mackenna, *Santiago,* I, 351-352, II, 389-391; Amunátegui Solar, *Mayorazgos,* III, 280-281, *Historia social de Chile,* 180-181, and "Trata," 31-32; Vial Correa, *Africano,* 37-43, 49-50.

[27]Marquez de la Plata, "Trajes," provides a thorough discussion of upper class apparel; Gómez de Vidaurre, II, 305-306, describes fashions in the later eighteenth century; Vicuña Mackenna, *Santiago,* II, 367-369, reproduces an eighteenth-century draft for a dowry receipt which mentioned but did not specify dressmaking costs for trousseau items.

[28]Vial Correa, *Africano,* 30-31.

[29]*Actas,* XXXIII, 89, 112, 119 (1646: Feb. 20, June 22; Aug. 31).

[30]*Ibid.,* XXIV, 181, 183, 209-210, 220, 249-250, 277-279, 283, 285 (1610: July 9, 23; 1611: Jan. 5, 24; May 2; Sept. 13, 16, 23, 30); XXVIII, 150, 169 (1623: Aug. 18; Nov. 10); XXX, 194, 234, 241, 265-266, 294 (1630: Aug. 30; Nov. 3; Dec. 23; 1631: June 20; Oct. 31); XXXI, 86-87, 162 (1635: March 8; 1636: Feb. 1).

[31]Amunátegui Solar, *Cabildo de la Serena,* 23, 43, 150-152, 155-160; Concha, 83-84; *Actas,* XLVII, 10, 76, 137 (1710: Jan. 7; 1711: Jan. 7; 1712: Jan. 7); L, 247, 287, 336 (1720: Jan. 8; 1721: Jan. 10; 1722: Jan. 7). See also "Actas, 1707," *RCHG,* no. 79, 481, "Actas, 1708," *ibid.,* no. 80, 735.

[32]Medina, *Cosas,* 88-90.

[33]"R. C. que los españoles vagamundos asienten y se ocupen en oficios," Madrid, Nov. 19, 1551, in Konetzke, I, 289-290, states that unemployed Spanish males were to be contracted to work for masters or to occupy themselves in other employment in order to support themselves. Those who did not go to work, if they were single, were to be deported back to Spain. "R. C. que los mulatos y zambaigos sean criados en buenos costumbres y esten sujetos y ocupados en trabajos y oficios de provecho," San Lorenzo, Aug. 16, 1607, in *ibid.,* II, 134-135, speaks in a similar vein of nonwhites. See also *RLRI,* Book VII, title IV, laws 1-4.

[34]Jara, "Asientos," 21-95, especially 58; Sater, 26; Afro-Chilean females comprised 4.7 percent of the total of 516 contractual

employees.

[35]Góngora, *Encomenderos,* 207-211.

[36]Lillo, II, 357-359. When the sale took place, the king had just sent Governor Alonso de Sotomayor a special cédula ordering him to keep mestizos, mulatos, and blacks away from Indian lands, see "R. C. sobre que ningun mestizo, mulato ni negro este ni reside entre los indios," San Lorenzo, Sept. 5, 1584, in Konetzke, I, 554-555. This reenforced general legislation along the same lines, but encroachment on Indian lands by non-Indians obviously continued.

[37]Rosales, I, 465.

[38]Vial Correa, *Africano,* 43.

[39]*Actas,* XXXIV, 464 (1654: June 1); XLII, 410 (1691: Sept. 7); Flusche, "Public Health," 184-185.

[40]Matta Vial, 40 and note 2.

[41]Eyzaguirre, *Historia,* 382; Rout, 210-212; Sater, 35-36.

Part II:
Indias and Mestizas

[1]Bibar, 133-136, 155-156, 160-161. The *"ovejas"* that Bibar mentions were probably, in his day, the native South American stock. Gagliano, 103-107, studies the chronicler's identity. Eyzaguirre, *Historia,* 23-33, surveys preconquest Chileans and comments on the coming of the Incas.

[2]Rosales, I, 141-145; Tesillo, 23-24; Pérez García, I, 59-60; Gómez de Vidaurre, I, 310, 326.

[3]González de Nájera, 47-48.

[4]Núñez de Pineda y Bascuñán, *The Happy Captive,* tr. Atkinson, is an excellent translation of those portions of the classic work that recount the author's experiences during his captivity in 1629.

[5]Ovalle, 114; the short half-mantle rendered variously *lliclla, iclla,* and *iquilla* derived its name from the Quechua language, *ibid.,* editorial note 15. It was perhaps this piece of attire that notaries called the *lliquilla* in some inventories.

[6]Molina, II, 58-59, 64-65, 115-117; Gómez de Vidaurre, I, 314-315, 347-348.

[7]See, for example, Errázuriz, *Valdivia,* II, 484-487. A juridical definition of yanacona status is Solórzano y Pereyra, Book II, chap.

IV.

[8]"Testamento de Juan Ruiz de León," Santiago, Oct. 11, 1590, in
DI, 2nd ser., VI, 317-319, includes bequests to Indian servitors. The
peninsular testator, a resident of Valdivia, bequeathed each male
yanacona two garments. The wives of the yanaconas were each to have
one garment, and the Indians as a group were to receive ten sheep.
[9]Góngora, *Encomenderos,* 47.
[10]Góngora and Jara are among the Chilean historians who have
made important contributions to the history of the encomienda and
other questions regarding Indian status that are treated in this
prologue and in the ensuing chapters.

Chapter 3,
Abuses and Protective Measures

[1]Korth, *Spanish Policy,* analyzes the reforms undertaken and the
status quo of the Chilean Indians in the sixteenth and seventeenth
centuries.
[2]'Título de encomienda de Pedro de Maluenda,' Santiago, Aug. 18,
1584, in Allende Navarro, 161-163, is an example.
[3]Korth, 25-26, 29-30; Errázuriz, *Valdivia,* I, 183-184, and his *García
de Mendoza,* 442-443; Mariño de Lobera, 260-262; *Actas,* I, 284-291;
471-472 (1552: Jan. 2, March 4; 1555: Feb. 15, 22).
[4]Hernando de Santillán, "Ordenanzas para la Concepción,
Imperial, Cañete, Valdivia; Villarrica y Osorno," Valparaíso, June 4,
1559, in *DI,* 1st ser., XXVIII, 297-302, and his "Relación de lo que el
licenciado Hernando de Santillán, oidor de la audiencia de Lima
proveyó para el buen gobierno y pacificación y defensa del reino de
Chile," June 4, 1559, in *ibid.,* 284-297; Korth, 23, 31-39; Jara, *Salario,*
96-98, and *passim.*
[5]"Carta de fray Diego de Medellín a Su Majestad sobre el estado de
la religión en el obispado y calamidades que produce la guerra,"
Santiago, April 15, 1580, in *DI,* 2nd ser., III, 35-38; Korth, 67.
[6]Ramón, "Encomienda de Juan de Cuevas," 68-102.
[7]*Ibid.,* 102-107.
[8]*Ibid.,* 59-60.
[9]Korth, 68-71; Jara, *Salario,* 22-24, 62-63; "Tasa y ordenanza para
los indios hecha por Martín Ruiz de Gamboa," Santiago, May 8, 1580,

in *DI,* 2nd ser., III, 58-68; the new legislation explicitly forbade encomenderos from forcing any india to work for them without an express license from the governor and chief justice, *ibid.,* 61-62, 66. Solórzano y Pereyra, Book II, chap. II, treats personal service.

[10]'Ordenanzas y auto de Alonso de Sotomayor (fragmentos),' Santiago, Oct. 1, 1584, and March 8, 1589, in Góngora, "Documentos inéditos," [part I], 219-221; Korth, 71-73; Jara, *Salario,* 24-25; the restoration of personal service was in direct contravention of a decree Philip II addressed to Sotomayor from Lisbon on Sept. 24, 1581, reproduced in *ibid.,* 113.

[11]"Carta del cabildo eclesiástico de Santiago al rey sobre los abusos que se cometen con los naturales y criticando al gobernador Alonso de Sotomayor," Santiago, Aug. 10, 1588, in *DI,* 2nd ser., III, 422-424.

[12]Jara, 22-26, 62-64; Korth, 73-76.

[13]The discussion is based on "Ordenanza que deben guardar los administradores en los bienes de los pueblos de indios, dictada por el gobernador Martín García de Oñez y Loyola," Santiago, Feb. 4, 1593, in *DI,* 2nd ser., IV, 259-267.

[14]"Instrucción y ordenanza de lo que deben guardar los protectores de indios, dictada por el gobernador Martín García de Oñez y Loyola," Santiago, Feb. 4, 1593, in *ibid.,* 267-273.

[15]"Provisión del gobernador Martín García de Oñez y Loyola acerca del buen tratamiento que se ha de dar a los indios," Concepción, June 20, 1593, in *ibid.,* 333-335.

[16]Bishop Cisneros to Philip II, Dec. 17, 1590, in Amunátegui Solar, *Encomiendas,* I, 285-286; Korth, 74-75.

[17]*Ibid.,* 75-76.

[18]'Alquileres y ventas de indios, 1599-1620,' in Jara, "Fuentes," III, 131-135, reproduces the cession and bills of sale of female war prisoners.

[19]Cédula of Philip III to the governor of Chile, Ventosilla, May 26, 1608, AAS, vol. LVII, 151; Korth, 84-85, 117-119, 150-152, 156, 163-164, 177, 191-192; Eyzaguirre, *Historia,* 85-86, 91-92, 95-96, 155-156, 173-174. Executive orders implementing the slavery decree are reproduced in *Actas,* XXIV, 188-191 (1610: Aug. 20, Sept. 13).

[20]Eyzaguirre, *Historia,* 156-158; Korth, 111, 130-131, 156-157.

[21]*Ibid.,* 115-116, 161. The reaffirmation of slavery, dated Madrid, July 17, 1622, is in *DAAS,* II, 481-485.

[22]Korth, 174-175.

[23]Cédula of the Queen Regent Mariana to Governor Juan Henríquez, Madrid, Dec. 20, 1674, AAS, vol. LVII, 203-208 v. See

also *RLRI,* Book VI, title II, laws 14, 16; Consulta of the Council of the Indies and royal decrees in Konetzke, II, 603-612, 675-679, 749-752, 789-790; Korth, 192-203; Eyzaguirre, *Historia,* 174.

[24]Korth, 155-156, 163-164, 177-181, 189-191.

[25]Antonio Ramírez de Laguna to the king, Santiago, June 30, 1652, in Amunátegui Solar, *Encomiendas,* II, 53-55; Góngora, *Encomenderos,* 67. It was reported that purchases continued to be made as late as 1699, Bishop Francisco de la Puebla González to the king, Santiago, Sept. 20, 1699, in *DAAS,* I, 425-426.

[26]"Real cédula al obispo de Santiago en que se le ruega y encarga advocarse la causa de una india llamada Margarita," in *ibid.,* III, 277-280. It is reasonable to assume that the impetus for the decree, signed with the customary I THE KING in Madrid on Dec. 5, 1675, came from Queen Mother Mariana; see Lynch, II, 240-242.

[27]Diego Vibanco, captain of cavalry, to the king, Oct. 18, 1656, in Gay, II, 417-421.

[28]Korth, 103-116, 167-177, 207-208.

[29]Tasa of Esquilache, in *BHC,* I, 134-151; Korth, 110-114. Persons legally enslaved from Aug., 1610, to March 29, 1612, would continue to be slaves, but others would be manumitted.

[30]'Autos sobre la Tasa de Esquilache,' in Góngora, "Documentos inéditos," (Continuación), 150-176; Korth, 114-116.

[31]Royal ordinances relieving the Chilean Indians of personal service and authorizing enslavement of captives, Madrid, July 17, 1622, in *DAAS,* II, 480-516; Korth, 115-116, 161; Eyzaguirre, *Historia,* 177. The digest of the royal tasa in *RLRI,* Book VI, title XVI, deletes the clauses on slavery because the abolition decree predated the *RLRI.*

[32]Góngora, "Notas," 27-38; Korth, 167-174. The new ordinances amplified the royal tasa; hence the two existed side by side.

[33]"Tasa y ordenanzas que ha hecho don Francisco Laso de la Vega, presidente, gobernador y capitán general del reino de Chile, para el desagravio de los indios naturales del, en virtud de cédula real de Su Majestad,' Santiago, April 16, 1635, in Jara, "Fuentes," I, 119-133.

[34]*RLRI,* Book VI, title XVI.

[35]*Synodo 1688.*

[36]*Ibid.,* Chap. IV, constitution II.

[37]*Ibid.,* Chap. X, constitution III.

[38]*Ibid.,* constitution II. Some of the lusitanas may, of course, actually have been Portuguese women.

[39]*Ibid.,* Chap. IV, constitution IV; Chap. V; Chap. IX, constitution VII.

NOTES

[40]*Ibid.,* Chap. IV, constitution III.

[41]*Ibid.,* constitution V, and Chap. IX, constitution I.

[42]*Ibid.,* Chap. IV, constitution XII.

[43]*Actas,* XLII, 240, 252, 265-267 (1687: Nov. 7; 1688: Jan. 16, 23); Flusche, "Councilmen and the Church," 178-181.

[44]*Synodo 1688,* Chap. IV, constitutions VI, XV-XVII; Chap. IX, constitutions VIII-X. The stole fees set in 1632 for the Spanish towns and cities in the diocese were republished in 1689 following the synod, *ibid.,* 112-117. *RLRI,* Book VI, title XVI, laws 12, 14-15, called for a priestly stipend to be deducted from Indian tribute; since encomenderos still collected tribute in personal service, they had to make the monetary payments for priests who worked among the Indians, *ibid.,* laws 25-26, 32, 39, 49-50, 54, 57, 60, 65-66.

[45]*Actas,* XLII, 266 (1688: Jan. 23).

[46]*Synodo 1688,* Chap. III, constitution II; Chap. IV, constitution I.

[47]*Ibid.,* Chap. IV, constitution X. The crown had reprimanded the bishop of Concepción in 1630 for a lax attitude toward Indian marriages, Royal cédula to the bishop of Concepción, Madrid, Aug. 29, 1630, in *DAAS,* II, 536-538; related decrees are in *ibid.,* 522-525, 538-543.

[48]*Synodo 1688,* Chap. IV, constitutions XI, XVIII. The baptismal records were to list Spaniards in one book and Indians, mestizos, blacks, and mulatos in another. The marital registry was to show weddings and nuptial blessings.

[49]*Ibid.,* Chap. IX, constitution VI. Ecclesiastics in Santiago in the sixteenth century spoke in support of the right of Indians to marry freely, "Memorial de algunas cosas que parece ser necesario . . ." Santiago, *ca.* 1584-1588, *DI,* 2nd ser., III, 217.

[50]*Synodo 1688,* Chap. IX, constitution IV; Chap. X, constitution V.

[51]Flusche, "Councilmen and the Church," 177-179.

[52]*Synodo 1688,* Chap. IV, constitution VII; Chap. IX, constitution II.

[53]Royal cédula ordering the observation of the laws prohibiting the personal service of Chilean Indians, Madrid, July 16, 1700, in Konetzke, III, 80-81.

[54]"Consulta del Consejo de las Indias sobre la reducción de los indios en Chile," Madrid, April 29, 1703, in *ibid.,* 89-92; the Council cited the bishop's letter of Jan. 9, 1700, reporting on abuses.

[55]Royal cédulas addressed to the cathedral chapter and the bishop of Santiago on the reduction of Indians to pueblos, Buen Retiro, June 14, 1703, in *DAAS,* IV, 115-119. See also Góngora, "Notas," 44-51.

[56]Korth, 208.

[57]Amunátegui Solar, *Encomiendas*, II, 3-5, 9-13.

[58]'Tasa,' in Jara, "Fuentes," I, 126.

[59]Amunátegui, 402. Isabel was Lorenza's aunt. A similar suit was lodged against Agustín Ramírez for mistreating an india in Cuyo in the 1680s, "Juicio seguido a D. Agustín Ramírez por maltrato a una india en San Juan," in Espejo, *Cuyo,* I, 290.

[60]Góngora, "Notas," 38-44.

[61]*Ibid.,* 50-51.

[62]*Actas,* XXX, 156-158 (1630: Feb. 23), summarizes the documentation and notes that Alonso's bondsman was Cristóbal Hernández del Alamo. Governor Lazo de la Vega appointed San Juan de Hermúa as the protector of Indians to whom the several administrators of Indian pueblos had to report, *ibid.,* 211-215, 217-219 (1630: Sept. 16, 23).

[63]Amunátegui Solar, *Mayorazgos,* I, 280, 286, 295-296, 302-308, 315-316; Góngora, *Encomenderos,* 148, 174, 185-186.

[64]Bishop Francisco de Salcedo to the king, Santiago, Jan. 30, 1630, in *DAAS,* I, 137-141.

[65]Espejo, *Cuyo,* I, 69-70, furnishes the pertinent data.

[66]Letters to the royal audiencia on the conduct of Juan de la Banda, corregidor of Cuyo, 1678-1679, in *ibid.,* 265-278.

[67]Góngora, *Encomenderos,* 191-192.

[68]Report on Juan Jufré de Estrada, in Espejo, *Cuyo,* I, 148-150.

[69]Lavrin, 35-36.

[70]Ovalle, 354-430; Rosales, I, 455-457, 466-469, II, 331; Olivares, *Compañía de Jesús,* 466-469; Amunátegui, 134, 142-143; Medina, *Cosas,* 194-195; Ramón, "Testimonio," 170-171.

[71]Medina, *Inquisición,* I, 267-273, 276-277 and note 9, 283-284, 300-302, 340-341, 391-399. Chile, as mentioned earlier, was under the jurisdiction of the Tribunal of the Holy Office in Lima; Indians were exempt from the Inquisition's jurisdiction.

Chapter 4,
Real Estate

[1]One of the more thorough recent studies is Borde and Góngora, see especially, I, 80-82, II, "Mapa predial, año 1604."

NOTES

2"Información contra el bachiller Rodrigo González, clérigo, residente en la provincia de Chile," Lima, Oct. 6, 1556, in *DI*, 1st ser., XXVIII, 57-68; Errázuriz, *Chile sin gobernador,* 429-460.

3Thayer Ojeda, "Apuntes," 204-205, 210, 222, and his *Santiago urbana,* 69, 160; Góngora, "Social Stratification," 447.

4Burkett, 101-128.

5Thayer Ojeda, *Santiago urbana,* 64, 68, 102-107.

6*Actas,* XLI, 66 (1681: Sept. 12).

7Lillo, II, 227-243. A Spaniard tried to stop the survey, but Governor Alonso de Ribera upheld Lillo's authority to continue measuring the Indian lands.

8Amunátegui Solar, *Encomiendas,* I, 151-152, II, 85-87, "Apuntaciones," 86-89; Góngora, *Encomenderos,* 9-11; Thayer Ojeda, *Santiago urbana,* 27, 48-49, 74-76, 107, 150; León Echaíz, 44-45. "Información de méritos y servicios de Bartolomé Flores," in *DI,* 1st ser., IX, 6-46, includes Valdivia's grant of encomienda to Flores.

9"Información de los servicios del capitán Pedro Lisperguer," in *ibid.,* XXIII, 23-31; Amunátegui Solar, *Encomiendas,* II, 87-95, "Apuntaciones," 74.

10*Ibid.,* I, 151-152, II, "Apuntaciones," 89-90.

11"Testamento de doña Agueda de Flores," Santiago, May 19, 1595, and "Cláusula testamentaria de doña Agueda de Flores," June 16, 1632, in Vicuña Mackenna, *Lisperguer,* 254-258.

12Lillo, I, 11-14, 101-111, II, 38-40, 243-245, 273-276, 371-373.

13*Ibid.,* II, 371-373.

14Góngora, *Encomenderos,* 149-150, 174, 182.

15Lillo, II, 239-241.

16Amunátegui Solar, *Encomiendas,* I, 310-312, *Mayorazgos,* III, 296-297, 321.

17Lillo, II, 204.

18*Ibid.,* I, 96-101; León Echaíz, 14-15, 38-39, 95.

19Góngora, "Notas," 46.

20Tomás de Azúa, fiscal protector of the Indians, to the king, Santiago, March 20, 1748, in Amunátegui Solar, *Encomiendas,* II, 58-66; "Informe de los oficiales reales al presidente de Chile," Santiago, March 2, 1759, in *ibid.,* 236-244.

21Sayago, 164-165. San Fernando's population totaled 109 persons in 1793: 44 men, 31 married women, 25 single women, 2 widows, and 7 children, *ibid.,* 218. Unfortunately, these figures are not readily comparable to the 1745 data that mention only those individuals entitled to land.

[22]Ramón, "Testimonio," 168-169.
[23]Amesti, 94-96, 104-105.
[24]Larraín, 55.
[25]Sayago, 84, 97-100, 103, 115, 316.
[26]*Ibid.,* 111, 362. The husband, Domingo Chacana, was from La Serena and the wife, Paula Nacamai, from Copiapó.
[27]Góngora, *Encomenderos,* 3-67.
[28]Góngora, "Notas," 45-46, 49-50.
[29]Amunátegui Solar, *Encomiendas,* II, 195-216.

Chapter 5,
The World of Work

[1]Deposition of Juan Jufré, in *DI,* 1st ser., XIV, 413-414.
[2]"Probanza de los méritos y servicios del general Juan Jufré en el descubrimiento y población de las provincias de Chile," in *ibid.,* XV, 5-216, incorporates papers pertaining to Constanza de Meneses and her son Luis Jufré, see especially 104-106, 188, and the Tasa of Martín Ruiz de Gamboa for the Jufré encomienda, 198-203.
[3]'Mandamiento de don Alonso de Sotomayor transformando una encomienda en indios yanaconas,' Angostura, March 30, 1590, in Góngora, "Documentos inéditos," (Continuación), 113-115, and his *Encomenderos,* 34.
[4]Lillo, I, 117-130; León Echaíz, 37-38, 41-43, 95-96; Góngora, *Encomenderos,* 36. Some Indians lived in Macul as late as 1797.
[5]Lillo, I, 125-127.
[6]Góngora, *Encomenderos,* 25-37; see also his "Documentos inéditos," (Continuación), 115-150, for 'Cuentas del obraje de Peteroa, 1597-1602.'
[7]Góngora, *Encomenderos,* 23-24, 49, 53-54; Jara, *Salario,* 72; Errázuriz, *Valdivia,* I, 183-184, and his *García de Mendoza,* 442-444.
[8]Rosales, I, 477-478; Góngora, *Encomenderos,* 18-19; Will of Beatriz de Guzmán, Santiago, April 20, 1596, in *BHC,* I, 342-345; Jara, "Asientos," 21-95.
[9]Governor Francisco Ibáñez y Peralta to the king, Santiago, Sept. 15, 1707, in Amunátegui Solar, *Encomiendas,* II, 209.
[10]Bishop Francisco de Salcedo to the king, Santiago, Jan. 20, 1630, in *DAAS,* I, 137-141, is an example.

[11]"Ordenanzas reales para la administración de los censos y bienes de las comunidades de indios,' Santiago, Nov. 11, 1647, in Jara, "Fuentes," IV, 169-181.

[12]Góngora, "Notas," 38-44.

[13]Korth, 26; examples of renting out Indians appear in 'Alquileres,' in Jara, "Fuentes," III, 102-111.

[14]Jara, "Importación de trabajadores indígenas," 177-212, and his "Asientos," 21-95; *Actas,* XXIV, 395-396 (1613: March 12).

[15]Jara, "Asientos," 34.

[16]*Ibid.,* 56, 90.

[17]*Ibid.,* 49, 51, 95.

[18]*Ibid.,* 55, 68, 94-95.

[19]*Ibid.,* 57, 68.

[20]*Ibid.,* 57, 90.

[21]*Ibid.,* 35.

[22]*Ibid.,* 40, 84.

[23]Amesti, 122-123, gives contracts from the 1630s.

[24]ES, vol. 89, protocols of Manuel de Toro Mazote, f126v, "Asiento de Juan, mulato, con Francisco, zapatero." Roa y Ursúa, 217, 401-402, identifies the notary and his uncle.

[25]ES, vol. 89, protocols of Manuel de Toro Mazote, f 110v, Contract of Luisa, india, with doña Ana Félix Cifontes. The contract, like many documents drawn up in seventeenth-century Santiago, used *patacones* rather than pesos to express the wages due in clothing. A *patacón,* like the silver peso, was equivalent to eight reales at that time; to simplify monetary references, we have therefore used the more familiar term pesos in such cases.

[26]Roa y Ursúa, 207, 217, 401-402, 477.

Chapter 6,
Beatriz Clara Coya:
Inca Princess and Chilean *Gobernadora*

[1]Burkett, 101-128, includes notice of Inca royalty and noblewomen. See also Lockhart, *Spanish Peru,* 209-213, and *Men of Cajamarca, passim.*

[2]Barros Arana, III, 188-189, 191 note 6, 223; Eyzaguirre, *Historia,* 95-96; Guarda Geywitz, 43; Molina, II, 251. The name of the new town

or fort is given variously as San Salvador and Santa Cruz de Coya.
[3]Garcilaso de la Vega, III, 253.

[4]*Ibid.*, 212-214, 240-254; Martín, 68-70; Vargas Ugarte, 221; Burkett, 104-106; Espejo, *Nobiliario,* 614-615.

[5]Viceroy Francisco de Toledo to the king, Oct. 21, 1572, in *DI,* 2nd ser., IV, 204; Title and act of possession of the encomienda granted to García [Oñez] de Loyola, Potosí, la Plata, and Arequipa, Feb. 10, Dec. 1, 1573, and Jan. 21, 1574, in *ibid.,* 204-215.

[6]Petition of Cristóbal de Maldonado to the king relating data on the suit with García de Loyola on the marriage of doña Beatriz Coya, n.p., 1577, in *ibid.,* 217-220; Presentation to the Council of the Indies referring to the marriage case, n.p., 1577, in *ibid.,* 220-222; García de Loyola to the king, Cuzco, March 20, 1590, in *ibid.,* 248-251; Garcilaso de la Vega, III, 252; Means, 134 note 8.

[7]Royal cédulas of Sept. 16, 1576, and Sept. 30, 1577, both in San Lorenzo, in *DI,* 2nd ser., IV, 233-235.

[8]Conditional grant of encomienda to García Oñez de Loyola by Viceroy Francisco de Toledo, Lima and Cuzco, 1578, in *ibid.,* 235-238. This encomienda had belonged to Beatriz de Figueroa, the widow of Pedro de Villagra, former interim governor of Chile; it is so identified in the document from the viceroy who noted the fact of her death.

[9]Letter of doña Beatriz Clara Coya, Cuzco, Aug. 4, no year, in *ibid.,* 241-242. She had written the letter to her husband in either 1578 or 1579; it bears her signature, *ibid.,* 224 and note 1.

[10]Copy of the lawsuit in the audiencia of Lima between the fiscal and García de Loyola on the fulfillment of the royal cédula granting him an income of 1,000 pesos and autos provided on it, 1582; García de Loyola to the king, Cuzco, March 20, 1590, in *ibid.,* 231-251. Oñez de Loyola held appointments as corregidor of the city of Potosí and interim governor of the Río de la Plata, but he never took office in the latter post, *ibid.,* 228-230, and *passim,* collects the documents.

[11]"Título de gobernador y capitán general del reino de Chile en Martín García de Loyola," San Lorenzo, Sept. 18, 1591, in *ibid.,* 252-255; "Petición de Martín García de Loyola al rey para que se le encomienden unos indios que tiene su mujer doña Beatriz Coya," n.p., June 11, 1592, in *ibid.,* 255-256. See also García de Loyola to the king, Cuzco and Lima, March 20, 1590, March 28, 1591, in *ibid.,* 248-255; Excerpt from letter of don Martín Henríquez, viceroy of Peru, to the king, Lima, Feb. 17, 1583, in *ibid.,* III, 189.

[12]"Párrafos de carta del marqués de Cañete a Juan de Ibarra, en el Consejo, pronunciándose en contra del nombramiento de Martín

NOTES

García de Loyola como gobernador de Chile," n.p., April 28, 1592, in
ibid., IV, 188-189; "Capítulo de carta del marqués de Cañete a su
majestad sobre el socorro que se acordó dar a Martín García de
Loyola," Callao, May 27, 1592, in *ibid.,* 256.

[13]Barros Arana, III, 189, 191 note 6.

[14]*Ibid.,* 234-235 and note 29; Roa y Ursúa, 424-425; Espejo,
Nobiliario, 614-615.

[15]Jara, *Salario,* 39-40, 66-67. Beatriz Clara owed 122 pesos and 4
tomines to the Indians.

[16]Vargas Ugarte, III, 22 note 5.

[17]*Ibid.,* II, 179, III, 22 note 5; Roa y Ursúa, 424-425; Juan's mother
was Juana de Borja y Aragón.

[18]"J.H.S. Las pretensiones que tiene doña Ana María de Loyola,
Coya, hija y heredera de d. Beatriz Coya, y nieta de don Diego
Sayretopa Yupangui, bisnieta de Mango Ynga, rebisnieta de
Guaynacap Ynga, señores que fueron de los reynos del Peru, y
heredera de todos los susodichos," in *BHC,* III, 37.

[19]Garcilaso de la Vega, III, 253-254; Roa y Ursúa, 424-425; Barros
Arana, III, 234-235 note 29; Espejo, *Nobiliario,* 615.

[20]"R.C. al virrey del Peru ordenándole informe sobre las
pretensiones que tiene el marqués de Alcañices y Oropesa cerca de que
se le continue el repartimiento de ciertos indios para sus obrajes y que
se le de la sobra de tierras del marquesado de Oropesa," Madrid, Dec.
31, 1671, in Konetzke, II, 571-573.

[21]A portion of the painting is reproduced in Eyzaguirre, *Historia,*
85.

[22]Rosales, II, 269, 271, 296, 303; Ovalle, 266, 276; Garcilaso de la
Vega, III, 252-254; Olivares, *Historia militar,* I, 272, 301-302; Carvallo
Goyeneche, I, 208, 219; Molina, II, 247-248; Gómez de Vidaurre, II,
169.

[23]Barros Arana, III, 234, citing a letter from a padre Riveros.

Conclusion

[1]The works of Lewis Hanke, including *The Spanish Struggle for Justice,* are major contributions to the literature on Las Casas; Korth, 1-21, establishes the background for the developing pro-indigenist campaign; Davis, 165-196, examines the arguments advanced for and against black people.

[2]Mörner, 45.

[3]Lockhart, *Spanish Peru,* 198.

[4]Gómez de Vidaurre, II, 283-284.

[5]Sater, 36-38.

[6]Burkett, 101-128.

[7]Socolow, 406 and note 12, cites the unpublished report of the Centro Latinoamericano de Demografía (Santiago, 1977).

[8]Rout, 323-326, utilizes Chilean data in his chronological table of prices.

Bibliography*

Primary Sources

Actas del cabildo de Santiago. 28 vols. In *Historiadores* and cited by the corresponding volume number of that *Colección.* Additional cabildo sessions for 1706-1710 are available in *RCHG,* nos. 78-82, 84 (1933-1935), *passim.*

Anon. "Memoria de los vecinos de Chile á quien Francisco de Villagra despojó de sus indios." In *Historiadores,* XXIX, 507-512.

Archivo del Arzobispado de Santiago. Vol. LVII. Royal cédulas.

Bermúdez Plata, Cristóbal, ed. *Catálogo de pasajeros a Indias durante los siglos XVI, XVII y XVIII.* 3 vols. Consejo superior de investigaciones científicas. Sevilla, 1940-1946.

Bibar, Gerónimo. *Crónica y relación copiosa y verdadera de los reynos de Chile.* Facsimile edition with a transcription by Irving A. Leonard. 1966.

Carvallo Goyeneche, Vicente. *Descripción histórico-jeográfica del reino de Chile.* 3 vols. In *Historiadores,* VIII-X.

Chile. Archivo Nacional. Archivo de los Escribanos de Santiago.

Clemence, Stella R., ed. *The Harkness Collection in the Library of Congress: Calendar of Spanish Manuscripts Concerning Peru, 1531-1651.* Washington, 1932.

Colección de documentos históricos recopilados del archivo del arzobispado de Santiago. Compiled by Elías Lizana M. and Pablo Maulén. 4 vols. 1919-1921.

Colección de documentos inéditos para la historia de Chile. First series. Edited by José Toribio Medina. 30 vols. 1888-1902.

Colección de documentos inéditos para la historia de Chile. Second series. Collected by José Toribio Medina. 6 vols. 1956-1963.

Colección de historiadores de Chile y documentos relativos a la

---

*Unless otherwise indicated, the place of publication of works in Spanish is Santiago, Chile.

historia nacional. Edited by José Toribio Medina *et al.* 51 vols. 1861-1953.

Espejo, Juan Luis, ed. *La provincia de Cuyo del reino de Chile.* 2 vols. 1954.

Fuero juzgo. In Martínez Alcubilla, *Códigos.*

Garcilaso de le Vega. *Historia general del Perú (Segunda parte de los Comentarios reales de los Incas).* Edited by Angel Rosenblat. 3 vols. Buenos Aires, 1944.

Gay, Claudio, ed. *Historia física y política de Chile: documentos sobre la historia, la estadística y la geografía.* 2 vols. Paris, 1846-1852.

Gómez de Vidaurre, Felipe. *Historia geográfica, natural y civil del reino de Chile.* 2 vols. In *Historiadores,* XIV-XV.

Góngora, Mario. "Documentos inéditos sobre la encomienda en Chile." [Part I.] *RCHG,* no. 123 (1954-1955), 201-224; Continuación, no. 124 (1956), 113-176.

González de Nájera, Alonso. *Desengaño y reparo de la guerra del reino de Chile.* In *Historiadores,* XVI.

[Huerta Gutiérrez, Juan de.] "Informe sobre doña Catalina de los Ríos." *RCHG,* no. 59 (1927), 133-141.

Jara, Alvaro. "Fuentes para la historia del trabajo en el reino de Chile." I, *BACH,* no. 54 (1956), 119-133; III, no. 58 (1958), 102-135; IV, no. 61 (1959), 156-181.

Konetzke, Richard, ed. *Colección de documentos para la historia de la formación social de Hispanoamérica, 1493-1810.* 3 vols. in 5. Consejo superior de investigaciones científicas. Madrid, 1953-1962.

Leyes de Toro. In Martínez Alcubilla, *Códigos.*

Lillo, Ginés. *Mensuras de Ginés de Lillo.* 2 vols. In *Historiadores,* XLVIII-XLIX.

Mariño de Lobera, Pedro. *Crónica del reino de Chile.* Edited by Francisco Esteve Barba. In *Biblioteca de' autores españoles,* CXXXI, Madrid, 1960.

Martínez Alcubilla, Marcelo, comp. *Códigos antiguos de España.* 2 vols. Madrid, 1885.

Medina, José Toribio, ed. *Biblioteca hispano-chilena.* 3 vols. 1897-1899.

Mendoza Monteagudo, Juan de. *Las guerras del Chile: poema histórico.* Edited by José Toribio Medina. 1888.

Molina, J. Ignatius. *The Geographical, Natural, and Civil History of Chili.* Translated by the English editor. 2 vols. London, 1809.

Núñez de Pineda y Bascuñán, Francisco. *The Happy Captive.*

Translated by William C. Atkinson. London, 1977.

Olivares, Miguel de. *Historia de la compañía de Jesús en Chile (1593-1763).* In *Historiadores,* VII.

_____. *Historia militar, civil y sagrada de Chile.* 2 vols. In *Historiadores,* IV, XXVI.

Ovalle, Alonso de. *Histórica relación del reyno de Chile.* Escritores de Chile, no. 1. 1969.

Pérez García, José. *Historia de Chile.* 2 vols. In *Historiadores,* XXII-XXIII.

Quiroga, Antonio de. "Memoria." In *Historiadores,* XXIX, 397-459.

Recopilación de leyes de los reynos de las Indias. 3 vols. Madrid., 1943.

Rosales, Diego de. *Historia general del reino de Chile.* Edited by Benjamín Vicuña Mackenna. 3 vols. Valparaíso, 1877-1878.

Las Siete Partidas. Translated by Samuel Parsons Scott. Chicago, 1931. The Spanish text is available in Martínez Alcubilla, *Códigos.*

Solórzano y Pereyra, Juan de. *Política indiana.* Annotated by Francisco Ramiro de Valenzuela. 5 vols. Buenos Aires, 1930.

Synodo diocesana 1688. Lima, 1764.

Synodo diocesana, que celebró el ilustrísimo señor doctor don Manuel de Alday y Aspee, obispo de Santiago de Chile, 1763. Lima, 1764.

Tesillo, Santiago de. *Guerras de Chile, causas de su duración y medios para su fin.* In *Historiadores,* V.

The Visigothic Code (Forum Judicum). Translated by Samuel Parsons Scott. Boston, 1910.

Secondary Sources

Allende Navarro, Fernando. "La ruina de Villarrica y la información de don Juan de Maluenda." *BACH,* no. 78 (1968), 152-197.

Amesti, Luis. "San Antonio de Malloa." *BACH,* no. 13 (1970), 93-123.

Amunátegui, Miguel Luis. *El terremoto del 13 de mayo de 1647.* 1882.

Amunátegui Reyes, Miguel Luis. *Don Antonio García Reyes i algunos de sus antepasados, a la luz de documentos inéditos.* 6 vols. 1929-1936.

Amunátegui Solar, Domingo. *El cabildo de la Serena.* 1928.

_____ . *Las encomiendas de indíjenas en Chile.* 2 vols. 1909-1910.

_____ . *Historia social de Chile.* 1932.

_____ . *La sociedad chilena del siglo XVIII: mayorazgos i títulos de Castilla.* 3 vols. 1901-1904.

_____ . "La trata de negros en Chile." *RCHG,* no. 48 (1922), 25-40.

Avila Martel, Alamiro de and Bernardino Bravo Lira. "Matrices impresas en un protocolo notarial de Santiago en el siglo XVI." *Revista chilena de historia del derecho,* no. 5 (1969), 163-178.

Barbier, Jacques A. "Elite and Cadres in Bourbon Chile." *HAHR,* 52 (Aug., 1972), 416-435.

Barros Arana, Diego. *Historia jeneral de Chile.* 16 vols. 1884-1902.

Borde, Jean and Mario Góngora. *Evolución de la propiedad rural en el valle del Puangue.* 2 vols. 1956.

Bowser, Frederick P. *The African Slave in Colonial Peru, 1524-1650.* Stanford, 1974.

_____ . "Colonial Spanish America." In *Neither Slave nor Free: The Freedmen of African Descent in the Slave Societies of the New World,* 19-58. Edited by David W. Cohen and Jack P. Greene. Baltimore, 1972.

Boxer, C. R. *Women in Iberian Expansion Overseas, 1415-1815: Some Facts, Fancies, and Personalities.* New York, 1975.

Boyd-Bowman, Peter. "Negro Slaves in Early Colonial Mexico." *TAm,* 26 (Oct., 1969), 134-151.

Briseño, Ramón. *Repertorio de antigüedades chilenas.* 1889.

Burkett, Elinor C. "Indian Women and White Society: The Case of Sixteenth-Century Peru." In *Latin American Women: Historical Perspectives,* 101-128. Edited by Asunción Lavrin. Greenwood Contributions in Women's Studies, no. 3. Westport, Connecticut, 1978.

Burkholder, Mark A. and D. S. Chandler. *From Impotence to Authority: The Spanish Crown and the American Audiencias, 1687-1808.* Columbia, Missouri, 1977.

Concha, Manuel. *Crónica de la Serena desde su fundación hasta nuestros dias, 1540-1870.* Serena, 1871.

Curtin, Philip D. *The Atlantic Slave Trade: A Census.* Madison, 1969.

Davis, David Brion. *The Problem of Slavery in Western Culture.* Ithaca, New York, 1966.

Díaz Meza, Aurelio. *Leyendas y episodios chilenos.* 4th ed. 15 vols. 1968-1969.

Errázuriz, Crescente. *Historia de Chile: Don García de Mendoza,*

BIBLIOGRAPHY

1557-1561. 1914.

_____ . *Historia de Chile: Pedro de Valdivia.* 2 vols. 1911-1912.

_____ . *Historia de Chile sin gobernador, 1554-1557.* 1912.

Espejo, Juan Luis. *Nobiliario de la capitanía general de Chile.* 1966.

Eyzaguirre, Jaime. *El conde de la Conquista.* Colección de estudios jurídicos y sociales, no. 14. 1951.

_____ . *Historia de Chile: génesis de la nacionalidad.* 2nd ed. 1964.

Florez Vicuña, Carlos. "El coronel don Pedro Flórez Cienfuegos." *RCHG,* no. 26 (1919), 159-162.

Flusche, Della M. "The Cabildo and Public Health in Seventeenth-Century Santiago, Chile." *TAm,* 29 (Oct., 1972), 173-190.

_____ . "Chilean Councilmen and Export Policies, 1600-1699." *TAm,* 36 (April, 1980), 478-498.

_____ . "City Councilmen and the Church in Seventeenth-Century Chile." *Records of the American Catholic Historical Society of Philadelphia,* 81 (Sept., 1970), 176-190.

Gagliano, Joseph A. "The Identity of Gerónimo Vivar." *The Newberry Library Bulletin,* 6 (March, 1964), 103-107.

Góngora, Mario. *Encomenderos y estancieros: estudios acerca de la constitución social aristocrática de Chile después de la conquista, 1580-1660.* 1970.

_____ . "Notas sobre la encomienda chilena tardía." *BACH,* no. 61 (1959), 27-51.

_____ . "Urban Social Stratification in Colonial Chile." *HAHR,* 55 (Aug., 1975), 421-467.

Guarda Geywitz, Fernando. *Historia de Valdivia, 1552-1952.* 1953.

Hanke, Lewis. *The Spanish Struggle for Justice in the Conquest of America.* Philadelphia, 1949.

Jara, Alvaro. "Los asientos de trabajo y la provisión de mano de obra para los no-encomenderos en la ciudad de Santiago, 1586-1600." *RCHG,* no. 125 (1957), 21-95.

_____ . "Importación de trabajadores indígenas en el siglo XVII." *RCHG,* no. 124 (1956), 177-212.

_____ . *El salario de los indios y los sesmos del oro en la tasa de Santillán.* 1960.

Korth, Eugene H., S. J. *Spanish Policy in Colonial Chile: The Struggle for Social Justice, 1535-1700.* Stanford, 1968.

Larraín, Carlos J. " 'Lo Arcaya' y tierras de Colina." *BACH,* no. 61 (1959), 52-90.

Lavrin, Asunción. "In Search of the Colonial Woman in Mexico: The Seventeenth and Eighteenth Centuries." In *Latin American*

Women: Historical Perspectives, 23-59. Edited by Asunción Lavrin. Greenwood Contributions in Women's Studies, no. 3. Westport, Connecticut, 1978.

León Echaíz, René. *Ñuñohue: historia de Ñuñoa, Providencias, las Condes y la Reina.* Buenos Aires, 1972.

Lockhart, James. *The Men of Cajamarca: A Social and Biographical Study of the First Conquerors of Peru.* University of Texas Institute of Latin American Studies, Latin American Monographs, no. 27. Austin, 1972.

———. *Spanish Peru, 1532-1560: A Colonial Society.* Madison, 1968.

Lohmann Villena, Guillermo. *Los ministros de la audiencia de Lima.* Publicaciones de la escuela de estudios hispano-americanos, no. 222. Sevilla, 1974.

Loveman, Brian. *Chile: The Legacy of Hispanic Capitalism.* New York, 1979.

Lynch, John. *Spain under the Habsburgs.* 2 vols. New York, 1965-1969.

Marquez de la Plata, Fernando. "Los trajes en Chile durante los siglos XVI, XVII y XVIII." *BACH,* no. 3 (1934), 29-97.

Martín, Luis. *The Kingdom of the Sun: A Short History of Peru.* New York, 1974.

Matta Vial, Enrique. "Apuntes y documentos para una biografía de don Agustín de Vial Santelices." *BACH,* no. 1 (1911), 29-48.

Means, Philip Ainsworth. *Fall of the Inca Empire and the Spanish Rule in Peru: 1530-1780.* New York, 1932.

Medina, José Toribio. *Cosas de la colonia, apuntes para la crónica del siglo XVIII en Chile.* 2nd ed. 1952.

———. *Diccionario biográfico colonial de Chile.* 1906.

———. *Historia del tribunal del Santo Oficio de la Inquisición en Chile.* 2 vols. 1890.

Mellafe, Rolando. *La esclavitud en hispano-américa.* Buenos Aires, 1964.

———. *La introducción de la esclavitud negra en Chile: tráfico y rutas.* 1959.

Mörner, Magnus. *Race Mixture in the History of Latin America.* Boston, 1967.

Ramón, José Armando de. "La encomienda de Juan de Cuevas a la luz de nuevos documentos (1574-1583)." *BACH,* no. 62 (1960), 52-107.

———. "Un testimonio sobre la situación de los indígenas de

BIBLIOGRAPHY

Aconcagua, Quillota y Choapa a comienzos del siglo XVII."
BACH, no. 60 (1959), 168-192.

Roa y Ursúa, Luis de. *El reyno de Chile, 1535-1810, estudio histórico, genealógico y biográfico.* Valladolid, 1945.

Rout, Leslie B., Jr. *The African Experience in Spanish America: 1502 to the Present Day.* Cambridge Latin American Studies, no. 23. Cambridge, 1976.

Sater, William F. "The Black Experience in Chile." In *Slavery and Race Relations in Latin America,* 13-50. Edited by Robert Brent Toplin. Greenwood Contributions in Afro-American and African Studies, no. 17. Westport, Connecticut. 1974.

Sayago, Carlos María. *Historia de Copiapó.* 2nd ed. Buenos Aires, 1973.

Silva i Molina, Abraham de. *Oidores de la real audiencia de Santiago durante el siglo XVII.* 1903.

Socolow, Susan Migden. "Marriage, Birth, and Inheritance: The Merchants of Eighteenth-Century Buenos Aires." *HAHR,* 60 (Aug., 1980), 387-406.

Tannenbaum, Frank. *Slave and Citizen: The Negro in the Americas.* New York, 1946.

Thayer Ojeda, Tomás. "Apuntes para la historia económica y social durante el período de la conquista de Chile, 1540-1565." *RCHG,* no. 38 (1920), 174-222.

———. "La familia del conquistador Juan de Cuevas." *BACH,* no. 16 (1941), 157-178.

———. *Formación de la sociedad chilena y censo de la población de Chile en los años de 1540 a 1565.* 3 vols. 1939-1941.

———. *Santiago durante el siglo XVI: constitución de la propiedad urbana i noticias biográficas de sus primeros pobladores.* 1905.

Vargas Ugarte, Rubén, S. J. *Historia general del Perú.* Edited by Carlos Milla Batres. 6 vols. Lima, 1966.

Vial Correa, Gonzalo. *El africano en el reyno de Chile: ensayo histórico-jurídico.* 1957.

———. "Aplicación en Chile de la pragmática sobre matrimonio de los hijos de familia." *Revista chilena de historia del derecho,* no. 6 (1970), 319-334.

———. "Los prejuicios sociales en Chile, al terminar el siglo XVIII: notas para su estudio." *BACH,* no. 73 (1965), 14-29.

Vicuña Mackenna, Benjamín. *Historia de Santiago.* 2 vols. In *Obras completas,* X-XI. 15 vols. 1936-1940.

———. *Los Lisperguer y la Quintrala (Doña Catalina de los Ríos).*

FORGOTTEN FEMALES

Edited by Jaime Eyzaguirre. 1944.

Index

INDEX

2, 38, 66.

Ibáñez y Peralta, Francisco, 60.
Indians: lifestyle of, 33-34;
 personal service of, 39, 43,
 46-47, 56, 59, 89 note 10;
 society of, 34-36.
Indian women: and Catholic
 religion, 37-40 *passim,* 44-46,
 50; economic occupations
 of, 28-30, 33-35 *passim,* 38-
 40, 43, 46-47, 58-63;
 enslavement of, 35, 41-43,
 90 notes 25, 29, 31; labor
 contracts, 43, 60-63, 70;
 legal regimen of, 5-8
 passim, 37-44, 46-49, 60,
 70; physical mistreatment
 of, 12, 47, 49; and real
 property, 39-40, 51-52, 54-
 57, 59; sexual exploitation
 of, 5, 35-36, 41, 49-50. *See
 also* Nonwhites.
Inquisition, Holy Office of the,
 19-20, 50, 92 note 71.
Irarrázaval y Bravo de Saravia,
 Antonio de, 27.
Irarrázaval y Zárate, Fernando
 de, 48.

Jara, Alvaro, 30, 41.
Jufré, Juan, 58.
Jufré, Luis, 58-60.
Jufré de Estrada, Juan, 49.
Justiniano, Catalina, 22.

Ladinos, 18, 24.
Las Casas, Bartolomé de, 69.
Lavrin, Asunción, 49.
Lazo de la Vega, Francisco, 7,
 43-44, 47, 48.
Lillo, Ginés de, 52, 54-55.
Lisperguer, Pedro, 36, 53, 62.
Lockhart, James, 69.
López de Zúñiga, Francisco,
 42.
Loyola, Ignatius, 66, 67.
Loyola y Coya, Ana María, 36,
 64, 66-67.
Lozano, María, 13.

Machado, Fernando, 63.
Machado de Cháves, Pedro,
 47.
Manco Inca, 65.
Margarita, 1, 77 note 1.
Mariana of Austria, Queen
 Regent, 8-9, 42.
Marín de Poveda y Azúa,
 María Constanza, 14-15, 81
 note 46.
Márquez, Margarita, 11.
Márquez, María Nicolasa, 11-
 12.
Marriage dowries, 21, 23-25,
 28, 48.
Martínez, Francisco, 56.
Martínez de Vergara, Gonzalo,
 56.
Mayorazgo (s), 21, 23, 27-28.
Medellín, Diego de, Bishop,
 38.

INDEX

Oñez de Loyola, Martín
García, 36, 39, 40, 41, 64-67.
Oropesa, Barbola de, 59.
Ortiz de Gaete, Marina, 61.
Osorio de Cáceres, Isabel, 25,
27.
Ovalle, Alonso de, 17-18, 33-
34, 67.

Pact of Quillín, 42.
Panigueni, Bartolomé, 52.
Peña Salazar, Juan de la, 42.
Pereira, Blas, 41.
Peruvian Indians in Chile, 34,
36, 51, 62, 64.
Philip II, 8, 65, 66.
Philip III, 67.
Philip IV, 43.
Pichunlien (Pico de Plata),
Mariana, cacica, 56.
Ponce, Ana, 31.
Ponce, Cristóbal, 42.
Ponce, Pedro, 31.
Ponce León de Varas, Isabel,
47.
Protector of Indians, v, 40, 47,
49, 56, 58, 66.
Puebla González, Francisco de
la, Bishop, 46.
Pulperías, 30.

Quiñones, María de, 30.
Quiroga, Antonio de, 14.
Quiroga, Rodrigo de, 14.
Quiroga y Gamboa, Inés de, 14.
Quismaichai, Ana, 56.

Recabarren Pedro de
Figueroa, Margarita, 24.
Recalde, Pedro de, 29.
Recopilación de leyes de los

reynos de las Indias, 8, 10,
43, 44, 70.
Reyes, Blas de los, 47.
Reyes, Tadeo de, 14.
Riberos, María de, 26.
Ríos, Catalina de los, 12, 53.
Ríos, María Mercedes de los,
13.
Rojas, Rosa de, 11.
Rolón, Elena, 31.
Rosa de Narváez, Pedro, 63.
Rosales, Diego de, 31, 67.
Rout, Leslie B., Jr., vi, 19-20.
Ruiz de Gamboa, Martín, 39,
58.

Sairi Túpac, Diego, 64, 65.
Santillán y Figueroa,
Hernando de, 38.
Sater, William F., 2, 71.
Serna, Elena de la, 15, 23.
Siete Partidas, Las, 4, 10, 13,
16.
Silva, María de, 19.
Sotomayor, Alonso de, 39, 58,
59.
Suárez, Inés, 18, 19, 55.

Tannenbaum, Frank, 4.
Tarabajano, Antonio, 2.
Tasa: of Esquilache, 43, 62; of
Gamboa, 39, 88-89 note 9;
of Lazo de la Vega, 43-44,
47, 90 note 32; royal tasa
of 1622, 41-46 *passim,* 90
note 31; of Santillán, 38.
Toledo, Francisco de, 65.
Toledo, Gonzalo de, 62.
Toro Mazote, Ginés de, 53.
Toro Mazote, Manuel de, 22,
62-63, 82 note 50.